Wedding Planning

Made Easy

From

WedSpace.com

Featuring DIY & Green Wedding Ideas

By Alex & Elizabeth Lluch
AUTHORS OF OVER 3 MILLION BOOKS SOLD!

WS Publishing Group
San Diego, California

Wedding Planning Made Easy
From WedSpace.com
Featuring DIY and Green Wedding Ideas

Written by Alex & Elizabeth Lluch
America's Top Wedding Experts

Published by WS Publishing Group
San Diego, California 92119
© Copyright 2010 by WS Publishing Group

Floral Research by:
Joan Hahn Perilla
Partner, Public Relations Marketing, Inc.
Marketing Consultant to the Flower Council of Holland

Design by:
Sarah Jang, WS Publishing Group

For Inquiries:
Log on to www.WSPublishingGroup.com
E-mail info@WSPublishingGroup.com

Printed in China

ISBN 13: 978-1-934386-93-4

CONTENTS

CONTENTS

Introduction

YOU MUST BE VERY EXCITED TO HAVE FOUND that special person with whom you will share the rest of your life. And you must be looking forward to what will be one of the happiest days of your life—your wedding! Planning a wedding can be fun and exciting, but it can also be overwhelming; that is why WedSpace.com created *Wedding Planning Made Easy*.

Wedding Planning Made Easy from WedSpace.com contains worksheets, checklists, timelines and comparison charts to keep you organized and on top of your wedding plans.

Wedding Planning Made Easy begins with a detailed wedding planning checklist containing everything you need to do or consider when planning your wedding and the best timeframe in which to accomplish each activity.

Next, a detailed budget analysis lists all the expenses that are typically incurred in a wedding. In this book, you'll find everything you need to know about each aspect of the wedding, including Options, Things to Consider, Tips to Save Money and more. In this updated edition, we have also included tips for making many aspects of your wedding eco-friendly. We are happy that more and more couples are interested in protecting the environment as they plan their weddings.

Wedding Planning Made Easy also includes wedding timelines for your wedding party as well as your service providers to help keep everyone on schedule.

We have also included detailed descriptions of ninety popular wedding flowers. We hope this helps you make the appropriate flower selection.

Wedding planning wouldn't be complete without a section to help you prepare for your honeymoon. This section will help you choose your ideal destination and develop a budget as you plan for the vacation of your dreams.

Finally, this new edition also includes a section on do-it-yourself — or DIY — wedding projects, which are a huge trend in weddings. DIY projects can often help couples save money and will add personal, memorable touches to their weddings. The brides and wedding professionals on WedSpace.com helped us put together 14 fun projects for crafty brides and grooms who want to include DIY, handmade elements.

We are confident that you will enjoy planning your wedding with the help of *Wedding Planning Made Easy*. Also, if you know other Options, Things to Consider, Tips to Save Money, or anything else that you would like to see included in this book, please write to us at: WS Publishing Group; 7290 Navajo Road, Suite 207; San Diego, California 92119 or email info@WSPublishingGroup.com. We will include your ideas and suggestions in our next printing. We listen to brides and grooms like you—that is why WS Publishing Group has become the best-selling publisher of wedding planners!

Sincerely,

Elizabeth H. Lluch

Considering a Green Wedding

THE ECO-FRIENDLY OR "GREEN" WEDDING has grown in popularity as couples are looking to protect the environment by choosing organic and recyclable options, as well as offsetting the impact their guests' travel will have on the earth. Having a green wedding makes a statement to your guests about the importance of protecting the earth from wear and tear.

Why Have a Green Wedding?

According to the group Climate Care, the average wedding emits approximately 14.5 tons of carbon dioxide (CO_2) into the atmosphere. Carbon dioxide is one of the main gases believed to be responsible for climate change and weddings emit a lot of it because of how resource-intensive they are.

The average wedding involves 100 to 150 people, each of whom must travel (either by plane, train, bus, or car) to the wedding site. Each of these consumes energy, but air travel is particularly hard on the environment, with each cross-country flight emitting 2.5 tons of greenhouse gases and using hundreds of gallons of nonrenewable fuel.

Before they left for their trip, guests were beckoned to the wedding by paper invitations, the production of which involved the felling of trees and the heavy use of water. Over the course of the wedding, massive quantities of energy are used to chill their drinks and flowers and heat their hotel rooms and food.

Even before the party started, pesticides were used to grow the flowers and produce, and the happy couple was sent gifts wrapped in extensive packaging and delivered by plane and truck.

Each of these activities releases pound after pound of CO_2 into the atmosphere (not to mention generating waste and trash, most of which is not biodegradable or recyclable). When you consider that the average person emits just 12 tons of CO_2 over the course of a whole year, it becomes clear that traditional weddings leave a heavy carbon footprint and are one of many events that could be contributing to climate change.

More and more, couples are looking for ways to offset the impact of their wedding on the environment, while still making their event beautiful and memorable. According to a survey by Condé Nast, publisher of *Brides* magazine, 60 percent of couples say it is important to consider the environment in their wedding; however, only 33 percent of couples surveyed were planning on having a green wedding. This indicates that while the majority of couples care about keeping their weddings eco-friendly, most aren't sure how to do so.

How Do I Plan a Green Wedding?

There are more options than ever for making your wedding eco-friendly! The wonderful thing about planning a green wedding is you can incorporate as many or as few green suggestions into your day as you want. You might host a small, eco-friendly group where your guests eat organic greens by soy candlelight and you don a hemp gown — but you can also stay fairly conventional by employing green twists on traditional wedding concepts. For example, you might simply serve a seasonal menu or buying locally grown flowers, even if they have been grown by conventional farming methods. How far you decide to take your green wedding is really up to you, your partner, your beliefs, and your budget.

Know that just because you decide to do a few things green doesn't mean you have to do everything green. Feel comfortable sending invitations printed on recycled paper but splurging on a dress made from conventional fabric. Revel in the freedom to serve a conventional menu but decorate your tables with reclaimed, handmade centerpieces. With so many options available to today's brides and grooms, there are a myriad of green combinations to apply to your wedding. Because we know that brides and grooms will want to pick and choose where they go green, the tips offered in this book provide a range of ideas, covering everything from small eco-friendly touches to intense green wedding overhauls.

Will a Green Wedding Be More Expensive than a Traditional One?

The average American wedding costs more than $20,000, and even more if there are multi-day events involved, such as a day-after breakfast. Collectively, Americans are spending more than $72 billion each year on getting married! Clearly, Americans don't mind opening their wallets when they say "I do."

One of the ways eco-friendly weddings evolved was out of an effort to cut down on this spending and the amount of waste associated with this special day. Instead of spending thousands on flowers that will be thrown out, couples opted to have their ceremony in a garden or other area equipped with beautiful foliage that doesn't need to be paid for, set up, or torn down. When they thought about all the food that would probably go to waste if plated meals were served, they opted for a lower-cost buffet arrangement, which saves copious amounts of food from being merely nibbled at. These are all good examples of how being eco-friendly is at times nothing more than just not using more than you need to.

Indeed, at the heart of the environmental movement is a commitment to simplification, conservation, and avoiding waste. Even if you don't buy a single organic product in the entire course of your wedding, you can have a green wedding if you simply reduce the amount of money spent on items that end up in the trash.

That said, some elements of an eco-friendly wedding will undoubtedly be more expensive than a traditional wedding. Serving an organic menu, for example, will likely cost more because food vendors charge a premium for high-quality food grown without pesticides. An organic wedding menu will cost between 10 and 15 percent more than traditional ones. Similarly, organic flowers tend to be around 2 to 10 percent more expensive than conventional flowers. Brides and grooms interested in incorporating these elements into their eco-friendly wedding can be prepared for these costs and borrow from elsewhere in their budget to cover them.

But it is a mistake to assume that "eco-friendly" necessarily means "more expensive." In fact, simply employing the reduce, reuse, recycle principle will save most brides and grooms quite a bit of money. For example, buying matching glass centerpiece vases from a retailer or party supply store can cost anywhere from $2.50 to $10 per piece. But you can craft lovely, unique centerpieces out of mismatched vases, glass bowls, and jars picked up at antique stores. For about $1 per piece, you can repurpose and reuse secondhand items for a vintage look.

Likewise, altering a dear relative's wedding dress or buying one secondhand can save hundreds of dollars, as could forgoing a traditional wedding cake and having a friend bake cupcakes from organic ingredients instead.

This book is filled with these kinds of tips that will help you reflect environmentally sound principles in your wedding, while possibly cutting costs and reducing the amount of waste your Big Day produces. When you see how simple it is to incorporate a few green touches into your wedding, you'll see why "eco-chic" is replacing "bigger is better" when it comes to many couples' weddings!

Sweet Memories

THE MOMENT SOMEONE SPECIAL PROPOSES is a memory that is cherished forever. The story will be told over and over, to friends, family, children, and grandchildren ...

How was your proposal special? Did he plan an elaborate scheme, or was it a simple, romantic display of his love for you? Did you propose to him? Every proposal is special and unique. You will have it forever, in your mind and in your heart.

Use the following pages to record that precious moment so the two of you can relive your memories together.

Answer the questions as you remember them. Let your words reflect the memory of each moment. Come back to these pages often as you plan your wedding. Reading about the day you got engaged will help to keep your romantic thoughts alive as you plan the event that will bind the two of you together for the rest of your lives!

THE PROPOSAL

Date: _October 24, 2010_

Time: _____

Location: _Stoney Creek_

Proposed by: _Shaun in a Geo Cashé_

He/she said/did:

_____

_____

_____

_____

_____

You said/did:

_____

_____

_____

_____

_____

_____

_____

Then we did/went to:

_____

_____

_____

_____

_____

_____

_____

My parents' reaction was:

....

....

....

....

....

....

His or her parents' reaction was:

....

....

....

....

....

My best friend's reaction was:

....

....

....

....

....

His or her best friend's reaction was:

....

....

....

....

....

....

WEDDING PLANNING NOTES

Wedding Events at a Glance

YOUR WEDDING WILL BE A CELEBRATION
that will most likely span several different events.
From the moment you get engaged to your last
dance, your wedding will be filled with
many special occasions.

Use the following worksheets to easily keep track of events, dates, locations, and contact information. Keeping these details in one place will help you plan ahead for each party and quickly reference important information.

Once you have finalized all of your events, make copies of these worksheets and distribute them to members of your wedding party, consultants, or vendors who would require this information.

WEDDING EVENTS AT A GLANCE

Engagement Party Date:

Engagement Party Time:

Engagement Party Location:

Contact Person: Phone:

Website: E-mail:

Bridal Shower Date:

Bridal Shower Time:

Bridal Shower Location:

Contact Person: Phone:

Website: E-mail:

Bachelor Party Date:

Bachelor Party Time:

Bachelor Party Location:

Contact Person: Phone:

Website: E-mail

Bachelorette Party Date:

Bachelorette Party Time:

Bachelorette Party Location:

Contact Person: Phone:

Website: E-mail:

Ceremony Rehearsal Date:

Ceremony Rehearsal Time:

Ceremony Rehearsal Location:

Contact Person: Phone:

Website: E-mail:

Rehearsal Dinner Date:

Rehearsal Dinner Time:

Rehearsal Dinner Location:

Contact Person: Phone:

Website: E-mail:

Ceremony Date:

Ceremony Time:

Ceremony Location:

Contact Person: Phone:

Website: E-mail:

Reception Date:

Reception Time:

Reception Location:

Contact Person: Phone:

Website: E-mail:

VENDOR INFORMATION AT A GLANCE

Vendor	Company	Contact Person	Phone #	Website/E-mail
Consultant				
Ceremony Site				
Officiant				
Reception Site				
Caterer				
Liquor Services				
Wedding Gown				
Tuxedo Rental				
Photographer				
Videographer				
Stationer				
Calligrapher				
Music: Ceremony				
Music: Reception				
Florist				
Bakery				
Decorations				
Ice Sculpture				
Party Favor				
Balloonist				
Transportation				
Rental Supplies				
Gift Suppliers				
Valet Services				
Gift Attendant				
Rehearsal Dinner				

Wedding Planning Checklist

THE FOLLOWING WEDDING PLANNING CHECKLIST itemizes everything you need to do or consider when planning your wedding and the best time frame in which to accomplish each activity.

This wedding planning checklist assumes that you have at least nine months to plan your wedding. If your wedding is in less than nine months, just start at the beginning of the list and try to catch up as quickly as you can!

Use the boxes to the left of the items to check off the activities as you accomplish them. This will enable you to see your progress and help you determine what has been done and what still needs to be done.

WEDDING PLANNING CHECKLIST

Nine Month & Earlier

❑ Announce your engagement.

❑ Select a date for your wedding.

❑ Hire a professional wedding consultant.

❑ Determine the type of wedding you want: location, formality, time of day, number of guests.

❑ Determine budget and how expenses will be shared.

❑ Develop a record-keeping system for payments made.

❑ Consolidate all guest lists: bride's, groom's, bride's family, groom's family, and organize:
1) those who must be invited
2) those who should be invited
3) those who would be nice to invite

❑ Decide if you want to include children among guests.

❑ Select and reserve ceremony site.

❑ Select and reserve your officiant.

Nine Months & Earlier (Cont.)

❑ Select and reserve reception site.

❑ Select and order your bridal gown and headpiece.

❑ Determine color scheme.

❑ Send engagement notice with a photograph to your local newspaper.

❑ Use the calendar provided to note all important activities: showers, luncheons, parties, get-togethers, etc.

❑ If ceremony or reception is at home, arrange for home or garden improvements as needed.

❑ Select and book photographer.

❑ Order passport, visa, or birth certificate, if needed, for your honeymoon or marriage license.

❑ Select maid of honor, best man, bridesmaids, and ushers (approximately one usher per 50 guests).

Six to Nine Months Before Wedding

❑ Select flower girl and ring bearer.

❑ Give the Wedding Party Responsibility Cards to your wedding party. These cards are published by Wedding Solutions and are available at major book stores.

❑ Reserve wedding night bridal suite.

❑ Select attendants' dresses, shoes, and accessories.

❑ Select and book caterer, if needed.

❑ Select and book ceremony musicians.

❑ Select and book reception musicians or DJ.

❑ Schedule fittings and delivery dates for yourself, attendants, and flower girl.

❑ Select and book videographer.

❑ Select and book florist.

Four to Six Months Before Wedding

❑ Start shopping for each other's wedding gifts.

❑ Reserve rental items needed for ceremony.

❑ Finalize guest list.

❑ Select and order wedding invitations, announcements, and other stationery such as thank-you notes, wedding programs, and seating cards.

❑ Address invitations or hire a calligrapher.

❑ Set date, time, and location for your rehearsal dinner.

❑ Arrange accommodations for out-of-town guests.

❑ Start planning your honeymoon.

❑ Select and book all miscellaneous services, i.e., gift attendant, valet parking, etc.

❑ Register for gifts.

❑ Purchase shoes and accessories.

❑ Begin to break in your shoes.

WEDDING PLANNING CHECKLIST

Two to Four Months Before Wedding

❑ Select bakery and order wedding cake.

❑ Order party favors.

❑ Select and order room decorations.

❑ Purchase honeymoon attire and luggage.

❑ Select and book transportation for wedding day.

❑ Check blood test and marriage license requirements.

❑ Shop for wedding rings and have them engraved.

❑ Consider having your teeth cleaned or bleached.

❑ Consider writing a will and/or prenuptial agreement.

❑ Plan activities for out-of-town guests both before and after the wedding.

❑ Purchase gifts for wedding attendants.

Six to Eight Weeks Before Wedding

❑ Mail invitations. Include accommodation choices and a map to assist guests in finding the ceremony and reception sites.

❑ Maintain a record of RSVPs and all gifts received. Send thank-you notes upon receipt of gifts.

❑ Determine hairstyle and makeup.

❑ Schedule to have your hair, makeup, and nails done the day of the wedding.

❑ Finalize shopping for wedding day accessories such as toasting glasses, ring pillow, guest book, etc.

❑ Set up an area or a table in your home to display gifts as you receive them.

❑ Check with your local newspapers for wedding announcement requirements.

❑ Have your formal bridal portrait taken.

❑ Send wedding announcement and photograph to your local newspapers.

Six to Eight Weeks Before Wedding (Cont.)

❑ Check requirements to change your name and address on your driver's license, social security card, insurance policies, subscriptions, bank accounts, etc.

❑ Select and reserve wedding attire for groom, ushers, ring bearer, and father of the bride.

❑ Select a guest book attendant. Decide where and when to have guests sign in.

❑ Mail invitations to rehearsal dinner.

❑ Get blood test and health certificate.

❑ Obtain Marriage License.

❑ Plan a luncheon or dinner with your bridesmaids. Give them their gifts at that time or at the rehearsal dinner.

❑ Find "something old, something new, something borrowed, something blue, and a sixpence (or shiny penny) for your shoe."

❑ Finalize your menu, beverage, and alcohol order.

Two to Six Weeks Before Wedding

❑ Confirm ceremony details with your officiant.

❑ Arrange final fitting of bridesmaids' dresses.

❑ Have final fitting of your gown and headpiece.

❑ Make final floral selections.

❑ Finalize rehearsal dinner plans; arrange seating and write names on place cards, if desired.

❑ Make a detailed timeline for your wedding party.

❑ Make a detailed timeline for your service providers.

❑ Confirm details with all service providers, including attire. Give them copies of your wedding timeline.

❑ Start packing for your honeymoon.

❑ Finalize addressing and stamping announcements.

WEDDING PLANNING CHECKLIST

Two to Six Weeks Before Wedding (Cont.)

❏ Decide if you want to form a receiving line. If so, determine when and where to form the line.

❏ Contact guests who haven't responded.

❏ Pick up rings and check for fit.

❏ Meet with photographer and confirm special photos you want taken.

❏ Meet with videographer and confirm special events or people you want videotaped.

❏ Meet with musicians and confirm music to be played during special events such as the first dance.

❏ Continue writing thank-you notes as gifts arrive.

❏ Remind bridesmaids and ushers of when and where to pick up their wedding attire.

❏ Purchase the lipstick, nail polish, and any other accessories you want your bridesmaids to wear.

❏ Determine ceremony seating for special guests. Give a list to ushers.

❏ Plan reception room layout and seating with your reception site manager or caterer. Write names on place cards for arranged seating.

The Last Week

❏ Pick up wedding attire and make sure everything fits.

❏ Do final guest count and notify your caterer or reception site manager.

❏ Gather everything you will need for the rehearsal and wedding day

❏ Arrange for someone to drive the getaway car.

❏ Review the schedule of events and last minute arrangements with your service providers. Give them each a detailed timeline.

❏ Confirm all honeymoon reservations and accommodations. Pick up tickets and traveler's checks.

❏ Finish packing your suitcases for the honeymoon.

❏ Familiarize yourself with guests' names. It will help during the receiving line and reception.

❏ Notify the post office to hold mail while you are on your honeymoon.

❑ Review list of things to bring to the rehearsal

❑ Put suitcases in getaway car.

❑ Give your bridesmaids the lipstick, nail polish, and accessories you want them to wear for the wedding.

❑ Give best man the officiant's fee and any other checks for service providers. Instruct him to deliver these checks the day of the wedding.

❑ Arrange for someone to bring accessories such as flower basket, ring pillow, guest book and pen, toasting glasses, cake cutting knife, and napkins to the ceremony and reception.

❑ Arrange for someone to mail announcements the day after the wedding.

❑ Arrange for someone to return rental items such as tuxedos, slip, and cake pillars after the wedding.

❑ Provide each member of your wedding party with a detailed schedule of events/timelines for the wedding day.

❑ Review ceremony seating with ushers.

The Wedding Day

❑ Review list of things to bring to the ceremony

❑ Give the groom's ring to the maid of honor.

❑ Give the bride's ring to the best man.

❑ Simply follow your detailed schedule of events.

❑ Relax and enjoy your wedding!

WEDDING PLANNING NOTES

Budget Analysis

THIS COMPREHENSIVE BUDGET ANALYSIS has been designed to provide you with all the expenses that can be incurred in any size wedding, including such hidden costs as taxes, gratuities, stamps, and other items that can easily add up to thousands of dollars in a wedding.

After you have completed this budget, you will have a much better idea of what your wedding will cost. You can then prioritize and allocate your money accordingly.

This budget is divided into fifteen categories: Ceremony, Wedding Attire, Photography, Videography, Stationery, Reception, Music, Bakery, Flowers, Decorations, Transportation, Rental Items, Gifts, Parties, and Miscellaneous.

At the beginning of each category is the percentage of a total wedding budget that is typically spent in that category,

based on national averages. Multiply your intended wedding budget by this percentage and write that amount in the "Typically" space provided.

To determine the total cost of your wedding, estimate the amount of money you will spend on each item in the budget analysis and write that amount in the "Budget" column after each item. Items printed in italics are traditionally paid for by the groom or his family.

Add all the "Budget" amounts within each category and write the total amount in the "Subtotal" space at

BUDGET ANALYSIS

the end of each category. Then add all the "Subtotal" figures to come up with your final wedding budget. The "Actual" column is for you to input your actual expenses as you purchase items or hire your service providers. Writing down the actual expenses will help you stay within your budget.

For example, if your total wedding budget is $30,000, write this amount at the top of the page 31. To figure your typical ceremony expenses, multiply $30,000 by .05 (5%) to get $1,500. Write this amount on the "Typically" line in the "Ceremony" category to serve as a guide for all your ceremony expenses.

If you find, after adding up all your "Subtotals," that the total amount is more than what you had in mind to spend, simply decide which items are more important to you and adjust your expenses accordingly.

Ceremony

- ❑ Ceremony Site Fee
- ❑ Officiant's Fee
- ❑ Officiant's Gratuity
- ❑ Guest Book/Pen/Penholder
- ❑ Ring Bearer Pillow
- ❑ Flower Girl Basket

Wedding Attire

- ❑ Bridal Gown
- ❑ Alterations
- ❑ Headpiece/Veil
- ❑ Gloves
- ❑ Jewelry
- ❑ Garter/Stockings
- ❑ Shoes
- ❑ Hairdresser
- ❑ Makeup Artist
- ❑ Manicure/Pedicure
- ❑ Groom's Formal Wear

Photography

- ❑ Bride & Groom's Album
- ❑ Engagement Photograph
- ❑ Formal Bridal Portrait
- ❑ Parents' Album
- ❑ Proofs/Previews
- ❑ Digital Files
- ❑ Extra Prints

Videography

- ❑ Main Video
- ❑ Titles
- ❑ Extra Hours
- ❑ Photo Montage
- ❑ Extra Copies

Stationery

- ❑ Invitations
- ❑ Response Cards
- ❑ Reception Cards
- ❑ Ceremony Cards
- ❑ Pew Cards
- ❑ Seating/Place Cards
- ❑ Rain Cards
- ❑ Maps
- ❑ Ceremony Programs
- ❑ Announcements
- ❑ Thank-You Notes
- ❑ Stamps
- ❑ Calligraphy
- ❑ Napkins/Matchbooks

Reception

- ❑ Reception Site Fee
- ❑ Hors d'Oeuvres
- ❑ Main Meal/Caterer
- ❑ Liquor/Beverages
- ❑ Bartending/Bar Setup Fee
- ❑ Corkage Fee
- ❑ Fee to Pour Coffee

Reception (cont'd.)

- ❑ Service Providers' Meals
- ❑ Gratuity
- ❑ Party Favors
- ❑ Disposable Cameras
- ❑ Rose Petals/Rice
- ❑ Gift Attendant
- ❑ Parking Fee/Valet Services

Music

- ❑ Ceremony Music
- ❑ Reception Music

Bakery

- ❑ Wedding Cake
- ❑ Groom's Cake
- ❑ Cake Delivery/Setup Fee
- ❑ Cake-Cutting Fee
- ❑ Cake Top
- ❑ Cake Knife/
  Toasting Glasses

Flowers

Bouquets
- ❑ Bride
- ❑ Tossing
- ❑ Maid of Honor
- ❑ Bridesmaid

CHECKLIST OF BUDGET ITEMS

Flowers (cont'd.)

Floral Hairpieces
- ❑ Maid of Honor/Bridesmaids
- ❑ Flower Girl

Corsages
- ❑ Bride's Going Away
- ❑ Family Members

Boutonnieres
- ❑ Groom
- ❑ Ushers/Other Family Members

Ceremony Site
- ❑ Main Altar
- ❑ Altar Candelabra
- ❑ Aisle Pews

Reception Site
- ❑ Head Table
- ❑ Guest Tables
- ❑ Buffet Table
- ❑ Punch Table
- ❑ Cake Table
- ❑ Cake
- ❑ Cake Knife
- ❑ Toasting Glasses
- ❑ Floral Delivery/Setup Fee

Decorations
- ❑ Table Centerpieces
- ❑ Balloons

Transportation
- ❑ Transportation

Rental Items
- ❑ Bridal Slip
- ❑ Ceremony Accessories
- ❑ Tent/Canopy
- ❑ Dance Floor
- ❑ Tables/Chairs
- ❑ Linen/Tableware
- ❑ Heaters
- ❑ Lanterns
- ❑ Other Rental Items

Gifts
- ❑ Bride's Gift
- ❑ Groom's Gift
- ❑ Bridesmaids' Gifts
- ❑ Ushers' Gifts

Parties
- ❑ Bridesmaids' Luncheon
- ❑ Rehearsal Dinner

Miscellaneous
- ❑ Newspaper Announcements
- ❑ Marriage License
- ❑ Prenuptial Agreement
- ❑ Bridal Gown Preservation
- ❑ Bridal Bouquet Preservation
- ❑ Wedding Consultant
- ❑ Wedding Planning Online
- ❑ Taxes

WEDDING BUDGET	Budget	Actual
YOUR TOTAL WEDDING BUDGET	$ 15,000.00	$
CEREMONY (Typically = 5% of Budget)	$ 750.00	$
Ceremony Site Fee	$	$
Officiant's Fee	$	$
Officiant's Gratuity	$	$
Guest Book/Pen/Penholder	$	$
Ring Bearer Pillow	$	$
Flower Girl Basket	$	$
Subtotal 1	$	$

WEDDING ATTIRE (Typically = 10% of Budget)	$ 1500.00	$
Bridal Gown	$	$
Alterations	$	$
Headpiece/Veil	$	$
Gloves	$	$
Jewelry	$	$
Garter/Stockings	$	$
Shoes	$	$
Hairdresser	$	$
Makeup Artist	$	$
Manicure/Pedicure	$	$
Groom's Formal Wear	$	$
Subtotal 2	$	$

PHOTOGRAPHY (Typically = 9% of Budget)	$ 1350.00	$
Bride & Groom's Album	$	$
Engagement Photograph	$	$
Formal Bridal Portrait	$	$
Parents' Album	$	$
Proofs/Previews	$	$

WEDDING BUDGET	Budget	Actual
PHOTOGRAPHY (CONT.)		
Digital Files	$	$
Extra Prints	$	$
Subtotal 3	$	$

WEDDING BUDGET	Budget	Actual
VIDEOGRAPHY (Typically = 5% of Budget)	$ 750.00	$
Main Video	$	$
Titles	$	$
Extra Hours	$	$
Photo Montage	$	$
Extra Copies	$	$
Subtotal 4	$	$

WEDDING BUDGET	Budget	Actual
STATIONERY (Typically = 4% of Budget)	$ 600.00	$
Invitations	$	$
Response Cards	$	$
Reception Cards	$	$
Ceremony Cards	$	$
Pew Cards	$	$
Seating/Place Cards	$	$
Rain Cards	$	$
Maps	$	$
Ceremony Programs	$	$
Announcements	$	$
Thank-You Notes	$	$
Stamps	$	$
Calligraphy	$	$
Napkins/Matchbooks	$	$
Subtotal 5	$	$

WEDDING BUDGET	Budget	Actual
RECEPTION (Typically = 35% of Budget)	$ 5250.00	$
Reception Site Fee	$	$
Hors d'Oeuvres	$	$
Main Meal/Caterer	$	$
Liquor/Beverages	$	$
Bartending/Bar Setup Fee	$	$
Corkage Fee	$	$
Fee to Pour Coffee	$	$
Service Providers' Meals	$	$
Gratuity	$	$
Party Favors	$	$
Disposable Cameras	$	$
Rose Petals/Rice	$	$
Gift Attendant	$	$
Parking Fee/Valet Services	$	$
Subtotal 6	$	$
MUSIC (Typically = 5% of Budget)	$ 750.00	$
Ceremony Music	$	$
Reception Music	$	$
Subtotal 7	$	$
BAKERY (Typically = 2% of Budget)	$ 300.00	$
Wedding Cake	$	$
Groom's Cake	$	$
Cake Delivery/Setup Fee	$	$
Cake-Cutting Fee	$	$
Cake Top	$	$
Cake Knife/Toasting Glasses	$	$
Subtotal 8	$	$

BUDGET ANALYSIS WORKSHEET

WEDDING BUDGET	Budget	Actual
FLOWERS (Typically = 6% of Budget)	$	$
Bouquets	$	$
Bride	$	$
Tossing	$	$
Maid of Honor	$	$
Bridesmaids	$	$
Floral Hairpieces	$	$
Maid of Honor/Bridesmaids	$	$
Flower Girl	$	$
Corsages	$	$
Bride's Going Away	$	$
Family Members	$	$
Boutonnieres	$	$
Groom	$	$
Ushers/Other Family Members	$	$
Ceremony Site	$	$
Main Altar	$	$
Altar Candelabra	$	$
Aisle Pews	$	$
Reception Site	$	$
Reception Site	$	$
Head Table	$	$
Guest Tables	$	$
Buffet Table	$	$
Punch Table	$	$
Cake Table	$	$
Cake	$	$
Cake Knife	$	$
Toasting Glasses	$	$
Floral Delivery/Setup Fee	$	$
Subtotal 9	$	$

WEDDING BUDGET	Budget	Actual
DECORATIONS (Typically = 3% of Budget)	$	$
Table Centerpieces	$	$
Balloons	$	$
Subtotal 10	$	$

TRANSPORTATION (Typically = 2% of Budget)		
TRANSPORTATION (Typically = 2% of Budget)	$	$
Transportation	$	$
Subtotal 11	$	$

RENTAL ITEMS (Typically = 3% of Budget)		
RENTAL ITEMS (Typically = 3% of Budget)	$	$
Bridal Slip	$	$
Ceremony Accessories	$	$
Tent/Canopy	$	$
Dance Floor	$	$
Tables/Chairs	$	$
Linen/Tableware	$	$
Heaters	$	$
Lanterns	$	$
Other Rental Items	$	$
Subtotal 12	$	$

GIFTS (Typically = 3% of Budget)		
GIFTS (Typically = 3% of Budget)	$	$
Bride's Gift	$	$
Groom's Gift	$	$
Bridesmaids' Gifts	$	$
Ushers' Gifts	$	$
Subtotal 13	$	$

BUDGET ANALYSIS WORKSHEET

WEDDING BUDGET	Budget	Actual
PARTIES (Typically = 4% of Budget)	$	$
Bridesmaids' Luncheon	$	$
Rehearsal Dinner	$	$
Subtotal 14	$	$

WEDDING BUDGET	Budget	Actual
MISCELLANEOUS (Typically = 4% of Budget)	$	$
Newspaper Announcements	$	$
Marriage License	$	$
Prenuptial Agreement	$	$
Bridal Gown Preservation	$	$
Bridal Bouquet Preservation	$	$
Wedding Consultant	$	$
Wedding Planning Online	$	$
Taxes	$	$
Subtotal 15	$	$

	Budget	Actual
GRAND TOTAL (Add "Budget" & "Actual" Subtotals 1-15)	$	$

Vendor	Contract Date & Total Cost	Deposit & Date	Next Pmt. & Date	Final Pmt. & Date
Consultant				
Ceremony Site				
Officiant				
Reception Site				
Caterer				
Liquor Services				
Wedding Gown				
Tuxedo Rental				
Photographer				
Videographer				
Stationer				
Calligrapher				
Music: Ceremony				
Music: Reception				
Florist				
Bakery				
Decorations				
Ice Sculpture				
Party Favors				
Balloonist				
Transportation				
Rental & Supplies				
Gift Suppliers				
Valet Services				
Gift Attendant				
Rehearsal Dinner				

WEDDING PLANNING NOTES

Ceremony

YOUR CEREMONY IS A REFLECTION OF who you are. It can be as simple or as elaborate as you desire. Many people choose to have a traditional ceremony in a church, while others have taken their special day outdoors to a park or the beach. These days, anything goes!

CEREMONY SITE FEE

The ceremony site fee is the fee to rent a facility for your wedding. In churches, cathedrals, chapels, temples, or synagogues, this fee may include the organist, wedding coordinator, custodian, changing rooms for the bridal party, and miscellaneous items such as kneeling cushions, aisle runner, and candelabra. Be sure to ask what the site fee includes prior to booking a facility. Throughout this book, the word church will be used to refer to the site where the ceremony will take place.

GREEN WEDDING TIP

Let Nature Be the Site of Your Wedding Indoor weddings require massive amounts of water, electricity, and air conditioning. Plus, they are typically plain spaces that must be brought to life with expensive and wasteful decorations. Therefore, aim to hold as much of your wedding outdoors as possible. Choose a site rich in natural beauty to minimize both your need to decorate and use a lot of energy. A garden in full bloom reduces the need to buy flowers, for example, as does a small beach near a quiet lake or a sprawling wildflower-filled lawn.

GREEN WEDDING TIP

Get Hitched In a Space that Maximizes Resources If your wedding must be indoors, choose an LEED-certified building. LEED stands for "Leadership in Energy and Environmental Design" and means the space has been sustainably built, conserves water and electricity, and may even run on renewable energy. LEED-certified spaces can be found at www.usgbc.org, the website of the U.S. Green Building Council. Also, if you choose a country club with a golf course, check to see if it is Audubon certified. This kind of course meets standards for conserving water and providing wildlife habitats.

Options: Churches, cathedrals, chapels, temples, synagogues, private homes, gardens, hotels, clubs, halls, parks, museums, yachts, wineries, beaches, and hot air balloons.

Things to Consider: Your selection of a ceremony site will be influenced by the formality of your wedding, the season of the year, the number of guests expected and your religious affiliation. Make sure you ask about restrictions or guidelines regarding photography, videography, music, decorations, candles, and rice or rose petal-tossing. Consider issues such as proximity of the ceremony site to the reception site, parking availability, handicapped accessibility, and time constraints.

Tips to Save Money: Have your ceremony at the same facility as your reception to save a second rental fee. Set a realistic guest list and stick to it. Hire an experienced wedding consultant. At a church or temple, ask if there is another wedding that day and share the cost of floral decorations with that bride. Membership in a church, temple, or club can reduce rental fees. At a garden wedding, have guests stand and omit the cost of renting chairs.

Price Range: $100 - $1,000

OFFICIANT'S FEE

The officiant's fee is the fee paid to the person who performs your wedding ceremony.

Options: Priest, Clergyman, Minister, Pastor, Chaplain, Rabbi, Judge, or Justice of the Peace. Discuss with your officiant the readings you would like incorporated into your ceremony. Some popular readings are:

Beatitudes	Corinthians 13:1-13	Ecclesiastes 3:1-9
Ephesians 3:14-19; 5:1-2	Genesis 1:26-28	Genesis 2:4-9, 15-24
Hosea 2:19-21	Isaiah 61:10I	John 4:7-16
John 15:9-12, 17:22-24	Mark 10:6-9	Proverbs 31:10-31
Romans 12:1-2, 9-18	Ruth 1:16-17	Tobit 8:56-58

Things to Consider: Some officiants may not accept a fee, depending on your relationship with him/her. If a fee is refused, send a donation to the officiant's church or synagogue.

Price Range: $100 - $500

OFFICIANT'S GRATUITY

The officiant's gratuity is a discretionary amount of money given to the officiant.

Things to Consider: This amount should depend on your relationship with the officiant and the amount of time he or she has spent with you prior to the ceremony. The groom puts this fee in a sealed envelope and gives it to his best man or wedding consultant, who gives it to the officiant either before or immediately after the ceremony.

Price Range: $50 - $250

GUEST BOOK/PEN/PENHOLDER

The guest book is a formal register that your guests sign as they arrive at the ceremony or reception. It serves as a memento of who attended your wedding. This book is often placed outside the ceremony or reception site, along with an elegant pen and penholder. A guest book attendant is responsible for inviting all guests to sign in. A younger sibling or close friend who is not part of the wedding party may be well-suited for this position.

GREEN WEDDING TIP

Involve Kimberley in Your Wedding The Kimberley Process was established by the United Nations in 2003. Its mission is to curb the trade of diamonds that are mined by rebel and terrorist groups and sold to finance war and human rights abuses in countries such as Angola, Cote d'Ivoire, the Democratic Republic of the Congo, and Sierra Leone. As of 2009, 75 countries were committed to the Kimberley Process, which requires that each diamond meet rigid requirements to make sure diamonds are mined, processed, and shipped in an ethical manner.

Options: There are many styles of guest books, pens, and penholders to choose from. Some books have space for your guests to write a short note to the bride and groom.

Things to Consider: Make sure you have more than one pen in case one runs out of ink. If you are planning a large ceremony (over 300 guests), consider having more than one book and pen so that your guests don't have to wait in line to sign in.

Price Range: $30 - $100

RING BEARER PILLOW

The ring bearer, usually a boy between the ages of four and eight, carries the bride and groom's rings or mock rings on a pillow. He follows the maid of honor and precedes the flower girl or bride in the processional.

Options: These pillows come in many styles and colors. You can find them at most gift shops and bridal boutiques.

GREEN WEDDING TIP

Twists on a Guest Book
Rather than wasting money and paper on a guest book, consider other ways to remember who attended your wedding. Have on display a large, handmade recycled paper panel that your guests can sign and you can frame. Or, get a signing platter. These plates come designed with your name and wedding date on them. Guests sign in, you bake the platter in the oven to seal the ink and keep it to use again and again. Check out www.guestbookplatters.com for different styles.

Things to Consider: If the ring bearer is very young (less than 7 years), place mock rings on the pillow in place of the real rings to prevent losing them. If mock rings are used, instruct your ring bearer to put the pillow upside down during the recessional so your guests don't see them.

Tips to Save Money: Make your own ring bearer pillow by taking a small white pillow and attaching a pretty ribbon to it to hold the rings.

Price Range: $15 - $75

FLOWER GIRL BASKET

The flower girl, usually between the ages of four and eight, carries a basket filled with flowers, rose petals, or paper rose petals to scatter as she walks down the aisle. She follows the ring bearer or maid of honor and precedes the bride during the processional.

Options: Flower girl baskets come in many styles and colors. You can find them at most florists, gift shops, and bridal boutiques.

Things to Consider: Discuss any restrictions regarding rose petal, flower, or paper-tossing with your ceremony site. Select a basket which complements your guest book and ring bearer pillow. If the flower girl is very young (less than 7 years), consider giving her a small bouquet instead of a flower basket.

Tips to Save Money: Ask your florist if you can borrow a basket and attach a pretty white bow to it.

Price Range: $20 - $75

GREEN WEDDING TIP

What's in Your Flower Girl's Basket? Keep this classic tradition but put an eco-friendly twist on it. Have your flower girl toss organic flower petals, or ask your florist to provide wilted petals from a wedding that occurred the day before yours. Or, skip flower petals entirely and have your flower girl toss unconventional items such as grass seed, a colorful assortment of dried leaves, shaved coconut, or biodegradable confetti. None of these need to be cleaned up and are safe for the environment and any animals that live at your wedding site.

CEREMONY SITE COMPARISON CHART

Questions	POSSIBILITY 1
What is the name of the ceremony site?	
What is the website and e-mail of the ceremony site?	
What is the address of the ceremony site?	
What is the name and phone number of my contact person?	
What dates and times are available?	
Do vows need to be approved?	
What is the ceremony site fee?	
What is the payment policy?	
What is the cancellation policy?	
Does the facility have liability insurance?	
What are the minimum/maximum number of guests allowed?	
What is the denomination, if any, of the facility?	
What restrictions are there with regards to religion?	
Is an officiant available? At what cost?	
Are outside officiants allowed?	
Are any musical instruments available for our use?	
If so, what is the fee?	

POSSIBILITY 2	POSSIBILITY 3

CEREMONY SITE COMPARISON CHART

Questions	POSSIBILITY 1
What music restrictions are there, if any?	
What photography restrictions are there, if any?	
What videography restrictions are there, if any?	
Are there any restrictions for rice/petal-tossing?	
Are candlelight ceremonies allowed?	
What floral decorations are available/allowed?	
When is my rehearsal to be scheduled?	
Is there handicap accessibility and parking?	
How many parking spaces are available for my wedding party?	
Where are they located?	
How many parking spaces are available for my guests?	
What rental items are necessary?	
What is the fee?	
Other:	
Other:	
Other:	
Other:	

POSSIBILITY 2	POSSIBILITY 3

CEREMONY READING SELECTIONS

SOURCE	Selection	Read By	When

WHEN	Selection	Composer	Played By
Prelude 1			
Prelude 2			
Prelude 3			
Processional			
Bride's Processional			
Ceremony 1			
Ceremony 2			
Ceremony 3			
Recessional			
Postlude			
Other:			
Other:			
Other:			
Other:			
Other:			
Other:			
Other:			

PERSONALIZED VOWS

Bride's Vows:

_____
_____
_____
_____
_____
_____
_____
_____

Groom's Vows:

_____
_____
_____
_____
_____
_____
_____
_____

Personalized Ring Ceremony:

_____
_____
_____
_____
_____
_____
_____
_____

PEW SEATING ARRANGEMENTS
Complete this form only after finalizing your guest list.

Bride's Family Section

• Pew _____

_____
_____
_____
_____
_____
_____
_____
_____

• Pew _____

_____
_____
_____
_____
_____
_____
_____
_____

• Pew _____

_____
_____
_____
_____
_____
_____
_____
_____

• Pew _____

_____
_____
_____
_____
_____
_____
_____

• Pew _____

_____
_____
_____
_____
_____
_____
_____

• Pew _____

_____
_____
_____
_____
_____
_____
_____

• Pew _____

_____
_____
_____
_____
_____
_____
_____

• Pew _____

_____
_____
_____
_____
_____
_____
_____

• Pew _____

_____
_____
_____
_____
_____
_____
_____

PEW SEATING ARRANGEMENTS

Complete this form only after finalizing your guest list.

Groom's Family Section

• Pew _____

_____
_____
_____
_____
_____
_____
_____

• Pew _____

_____
_____
_____
_____
_____
_____
_____

• Pew _____

_____
_____
_____
_____
_____
_____
_____

• Pew _____

_____
_____
_____
_____
_____
_____
_____

• Pew _____

_____
_____
_____
_____
_____
_____
_____

• Pew _____

_____
_____
_____
_____
_____
_____
_____

• Pew _____

_____
_____
_____
_____
_____
_____
_____

• Pew _____

_____
_____
_____
_____
_____
_____
_____

• Pew _____

_____
_____
_____
_____
_____
_____
_____

Unique Wedding Ideas

REGARDLESS OF YOUR RELIGIOUS affiliation, there are numerous ways in which you can personalize your wedding ceremony to add a more creative touch. If you're planning a religious ceremony at a church or temple, be sure to discuss all ideas with your officiant.

IDEAS TO PERSONALIZE YOUR CEREMONY

• Invite the bride's mother to be part of the processional. Have her walk down the aisle with you and your father. (This is the traditional Jewish processional.)

• Invite the groom's parents to be part of the processional as well.

• Ask friends and family members to perform special readings.

• Ask a friend or family member with musical talent to perform at the ceremony.

• Incorporate poetry and/or literature into your readings.

• Change places with the officiant and face your guests during the ceremony.

• Light a unity candle to symbolize your two lives joining together as one.

• Drink wine from a shared "loving" cup to symbolize bonding with each other.

- Hand a rose to each of your mothers as you pass by them during the recessional.

- Release white doves into the air after being pronounced "husband and wife."

- If the ceremony is held outside on a grassy area, have your guests toss grass or flower seeds over you instead of rice.

- Publicly express gratitude for all that your parents have done for you.

- Use a canopy to designate an altar for a non-church setting. Decorate it in ways that are symbolic or meaningful to you.

- Burn incense to give the ceremony an exotic feeling.

IDEAS TO PERSONALIZE YOUR MARRIAGE VOWS

- You and your fiancé could write your own personal marriage vows and keep them secret from one another until the actual ceremony.

- Incorporate your guests and family members into your vows by acknowledging their presence at the ceremony.

- Describe what you cherish most about your partner and what you hope for your future together.

- Describe your commitment to and love for one another.

- Discuss your feelings and beliefs about marriage.

- If either of you has children from a previous marriage, mention these children in your vows and discuss your mutual love for and commitment to them.

Attire

BRIDAL GOWNS COME IN A WIDE VARIETY of styles, materials, colors, lengths, and prices. You should order your gown at least four to six months before your wedding if your gown has to be ordered and then fitted.

In selecting your gown, keep in mind the time of year and formality of your wedding. It is a good idea to look at bridal magazines to compare the various styles and colors. If you see a gown you like, call boutiques in your area to see if they carry that line. Always try on a gown before ordering it.

BRIDAL GOWN

Options: Different gown styles complement different body types. Here are some tips when choosing your dress:

 GREEN WEDDING TIP

Sport a Secondhand or Vintage Outfit Employ the reduce, reuse, and recycle principle by wearing a secondhand or vintage outfit. The gown or suit can be easily altered to fit your body and style. When buying secondhand clothing, it's wise to exercise some caution. If possible, see the item in person to check for rips, stains, or irregularities. If the item will be shipped, don't be shy about asking for lots of photos from various angles. If possible, pay with a credit card or through a third-party payer in case you run into a problem.

Borrow a Gown or Suit from a Family Member Many brides and grooms of weddings past put the time, effort, and cost into preserving their wedding day outfit, only to never pass it on to a child or other relative. Take a brief survey of relatives in your family who were married at least 5 years ago. Someone might have the perfect gown tucked away, just dying to be worn again. Many eco-friendly couples like the fact that wearing a relative's old gown or suit is more personal and intimate than buying one over the Internet.

• **A short, heavy figure:** To look taller and slimmer, avoid knit fabrics. Use the princess or A-line style. Chiffon is the best fabric choice because it produces a floating effect and camouflages weight.

• **A short, thin figure:** A shirtwaist or natural waist style with bouffant skirt will produce a taller, more rounded figure. Chiffon, velvet, lace, and Schiffli net are probably the best fabric choices.

• **A tall, heavy figure:** Princess or A-line styles are best for slimming the figure; satin, chiffon, and lace fabrics are recommended.

• **A tall, thin figure:** Tiers or flounces will help reduce the impression of height. A shirtwaist or natural waist style with a full skirt are ideal choices. Satin and lace are the best fabrics.

The guidelines below will help you select the most appropriate gown for your wedding:

Informal wedding:
Street-length gown or suit
Corsage or small bouquet
No veil or train

Semiformal wedding:
Floor-length gown
Chapel train
Fingertip veil
Small bouquet

Formal daytime wedding:
Floor-length gown
Chapel or sweep train
Fingertip veil or hat
Gloves
Medium-sized bouquet

Formal evening wedding:
Same as formal daytime except longer veil

Very formal wedding:

Floor-length gown

Cathedral train

Full-length veil

Elaborate headpiece

Long sleeves or long arm-covering gloves

Cascading bouquet

Things to Consider: In selecting your bridal gown, keep in mind the time of year and formality of your wedding. It is a good idea to look at bridal magazines to compare the various styles and colors. If you see a gown you like, call boutiques in your area to see if they carry that line. Always try on the gown before ordering it.

When ordering a gown, make sure you order the correct size. If you are between sizes, order the larger one. You can always have your gown tailored down to fit, but it is not always possible to have it enlarged or to lose enough weight to fit into it! Don't forget to ask when your gown will arrive, and be sure to get this in writing. The gown should arrive at least six weeks before the wedding so you can have it tailored and select the appropriate accessories to complement it.

It's a good idea to put on "evening" makeup before going to try on dresses—trying on your wedding gown with a plain face is like trying on an evening dress wearing sneakers!

Beware: Some gown manufacturers suggest ordering a size larger than needed. This requires more alterations, which may mean extra charges. It is a good idea to locate a few tailors in your area and ask for alteration pricing in advance. Many boutiques offer tailoring services, but you will often find a better price by finding an independent tailor specializing in bridal gown alterations. Also, gowns often fail to arrive on time, creating unnecessary stress

 GREEN WEDDING TIP

Get Clothing Made from Organic Fabrics and Dyes There's nothing wrong with buying a new gown or suit, but make your purchase green by opting for clothing made from organic and fair-trade fabrics and with eco-friendly dyes or unbleached materials. Rawganique is one merchant that offers a wedding line made entirely from organic cotton, hemp, and linen. Threadhead Creations also offers stunning wedding attire made from natural fibers and lets you design your own outfit if you don't like their off-the-rack selection.

for you. Be sure to order your gown with enough time to allow for delivery delays and also be sure to check the reputation of the boutique before buying.

Tips to Save Money: Consider renting a gown or buying one secondhand. Renting a gown usually costs about 40 to 60 percent of its retail price. Consider this practical option if you are not planning to preserve the gown. The disadvantage of renting, however, is that your options are more limited. Also, a rented gown usually does not fit as well as a custom tailored gown.

Ask about discontinued styles and gowns. Watch for clearances and sales, or buy your gown "off the rack." Restore or refurbish a family heirloom gown. If you have a friend, sister, or other family member who is planning a wedding, consider purchasing a gown that you could both wear. Change the veil and headpiece to personalize it.

Price Range: $500 - $10,000

ALTERATIONS

Alterations may be necessary to make your gown fit perfectly and conform smoothly to your body.

 GREEN WEDDING TIP

Help Your Maids Get More Miles Out of Their Dresses Don't force your bridesmaids to end up like Katherine Heigl's character in the movie *27 Dresses*, who suffered with a full closet of only-worn-once dresses. Assign your bridesmaids gowns they will really want to re-wear. The best way to do this is to decide on a color, then have your bridesmaids choose their own gowns from any retailer they want. They are likely to choose a cut, style, and shade that really appeals to them, and the variation in their choices will make your wedding party interesting and unique.

Things to Consider: Alterations usually require several fittings. Allow four to six weeks for alterations to be completed. However, do not alter your gown months before the wedding. Your weight may fluctuate during the final weeks of planning, and the gown might not fit properly. Alterations are usually not included in the cost of the gown.

You may also want to consider making some modifications to your gown such as shortening or lengthening the train, customizing the sleeves, beading and so forth. Ask your bridal boutique what they charge for modifications.

Tips to Save Money: Consider hiring an independent tailor. Their fees are usually lower than bridal boutiques.

Price Range: $75 - $500

HEADPIECE/VEIL

The headpiece is the part of the bride's outfit to which the veil is attached.

Options for Headpieces: Bow, Garden Hat, Headband, Juliet Cap, Mantilla, Pillbox, Pouf, Snood, Tiara.

Options for Veils: Ballet, Bird Cage, Blusher, Cathedral Length, Chapel Length, Fingertip, Flyaway.

Things to Consider: The headpiece should complement but not overshadow your gown. In addition to the headpiece, you might want a veil. Veils come in different styles and lengths.

Select a length which complements the length of your train. Consider the total look you're trying to achieve with your gown, headpiece, veil, and hairstyle. If possible, schedule your hair "test appointment" the day you go veil shopping—you'll be able to see how your veil looks on your hairdo!

Tips to Save Money: Some boutiques offer a free headpiece or veil with the purchase of a gown. Make sure you ask for this before purchasing your gown.

Price Range: $60 - $500

GLOVES

Gloves add a nice touch to either short-sleeved, three-quarter length, or sleeveless gowns.

GREEN WEDDING TIP

Think Outside the Dress
Instead of wearing a formal gown or tuxedo, don an outfit you are more likely to wear again, rather than one that will end up collecting dust in a stored garment bag. Brides might find re-wear in a simple white sundress or tea-length dress. Grooms can choose a smart suit that can be worn to other weddings, job interviews, and formal occasions. Getting married in an outfit you will wear again helps conserve energy, money, and saves on chemicals used in the gown preservation process.

Options: Gloves come in various styles and lengths. Depending on the length of your sleeves, select gloves that reach above your elbow, just below your elbow, halfway between your wrist and elbow, or only to your wrist.

Things to Consider: You may want to consider finger less mitts, which allow the groom to place the wedding ring on your ring finger without having to remove your glove. You should not wear gloves if your gown has long sleeves, or if you're planning a small, at-home wedding.

Price Range: $15 - $100

GREEN WEDDING TIP

Avoid Polyester and Other Synthetic Materials
When purchasing clothes anew, avoid polyester, which is in most traditional wedding dresses. Making polyester is a resource-intensive process that requires a lot of water and energy. In addition, this synthetic fabric is made from petrochemicals, which are derived from oil and are a form of plastic. It takes hundreds of years for poly-ester to break down. Seek clothes that aren't made of this unfriendly material. Also, look for veils made of natural peace silk organza rather than nylon or tulle.

JEWELRY

Jewelry can beautifully accent your dress and be the perfect finishing touch.

Options: Select pieces of jewelry that can be classified as "something old, something new, something borrowed, or something blue."

Things to Consider: Brides look best with just a few pieces of jewelry—perhaps a string of pearls and earrings with a simple bracelet. Purchase complementary jewelry for your bridesmaids, to match the colors of their dresses. This will give your bridal party a coordinated look.

Price Range: $60 - $2,000

GARTER/STOCKINGS

It is customary for the bride to wear a garter just above the knee on her wedding day. After the bouquet tossing ceremony, the groom takes the garter off the bride's leg. All the single men gather on the dance floor. The groom then tosses the garter to them over his back. According to age-old tradition, whoever catches the garter is the next to be married!

Stockings should be selected with care, especially if the groom will be removing a garter from your leg at the reception. Consider having your maid of honor carry an extra pair, just in case you get a run.

Things to Consider: You will need to choose the proper music for this event. A popular and fun song to play during the garter removal ceremony is *The Stripper*, by David Rose.

Price Range: $15 - $60

SHOES

Things to Consider: Make sure you select comfortable shoes that complement your gown. Don't forget to break them in well before your wedding day. Tight shoes can make you miserable and ruin your otherwise perfect day!

Price Range: $50 - $500

HAIRDRESSER

Many brides prefer to have their hair professionally arranged with their headpiece the day of the wedding rather than trying to do it themselves.

Things to Consider: Have your professional hairdresser experiment with your hair and headpiece before your wedding day so there are no surprises. Most hairdressers will include the cost of a sample session in your package. They will try several styles on you and write down the specifics of each one so that things go quickly and smoothly on your wedding day. On the big day, you can go to the salon or have the stylist meet you at your home or dressing site. Consider having him/her arrange your bridal party's hair for a consistent look.

Tips to Save Money: Negotiate having your hair arranged free of charge or at a discount in exchange for bringing your mother, your fiancé's mother, and your bridal party to the salon.

Price Range: $50 - $200 per person

MAKEUP ARTIST

A professional makeup artist will apply makeup that should last throughout the day and will often provide you with samples for touch-ups.

Things to Consider: It's smart to go for a trial run before the day of the wedding so there are no surprises. You can either go to the salon or have the makeup artist meet you at your home or dressing site. Consider having him/her apply makeup for your mother, your fiancé's mother, and your bridesmaids for a consistent look. In selecting a makeup artist, make sure he or she has been trained in makeup for photography. It is very important to wear the proper amount of makeup for photographs.

Consider having your makeup trial right before your hairdresser trial—that way you'll see how your hair looks with your makeup on. It can make a big difference.

 GREEN WEDDING TIP

Look for Cruelty-Free Fabrics and Cosmetics

Make sure no animals were harmed in the making of your wedding by avoiding clothing made from traditional silk. Silk worms are often boiled alive or electrocuted in order to make this product. Instead, opt for "peace silk," which is made from a cocoon after the silk worm has hatched and left it behind. Also, only buy clothes that have been made by a company that is known to not use child labor or overseas sweatshops. Finally, beautify with cosmetics that were not tested on animals.

Tips to Save Money: Try to negotiate having your makeup applied free of charge or at a discount in exchange for bringing your mother, your fiancé's mother, and your wedding party to the salon.

Price Range: $30 - $150 per person

MANICURE/PEDICURE

As a final touch, it's nice to have a professional manicure and/or pedicure the day of your wedding.

Things to Consider: Don't forget to bring the appropriate color nail polish with you for your appointment. You can either go to the salon or have the manicurist meet you at your home or dressing site. Consider having him/her give your mother, your fiancé's mother, and your bridesmaids a manicure in the same color.

Tips to Save Money: Try to negotiate getting a manicure or pedicure free of charge or at a discount in exchange for bringing your mother, your fiancé's mother, and your wedding party to the salon.

Price Range: $15 - $75 per person

GROOM'S FORMAL WEAR

The groom should select his formal wear based on the formality of the wedding. For a semiformal or formal wedding, the groom will need a tuxedo. A tuxedo is the formal jacket worn by men on special or formal occasions. The most popular colors are black, white, and gray.

Options: Use the following guidelines to select customary attire for the groom:

Informal wedding:
Business suit
White dress shirt and tie

Semiformal daytime:
Formal suit
White dress shirt
Cummerbund or vest
Four-in-hand or bow tie

Semiformal evening:
Formal suit or dinner jacket
Matching trousers
White shirt

GREEN WEDDING TIP

Cut Down on One-Time-Use Items A money-saving way to keep your wedding party green is to refrain from making your groomsmen and bridesmaids buy items they will only use at your wedding. For example, let bridesmaids buy black, silver, or gold shoes they will re-wear, rather than asking them to get dyed matching ones. Avoid requiring maids to carry purses, scarves, parasols, or other items that don't match any other outfit in nature. If there is an item you want everyone to have, see if it can be rented for the affair.

Cummerbund or vest
Black bow tie
Cuff links and studs

Very formal daytime:
Cutaway coat
Wing-collared shirt
Ascot
Striped trousers
Cuff links
Gloves

Very formal evening:
Black tailcoat
Matching striped trousers
Bow tie
White wing-collared shirt
Waistcoat
Patent leather shoes
Studs and cuff links
Gloves

GREEN WEDDING TIP

Donate Your Wedding Dress
It is romantic to think of your daughter one day walking down the aisle in the gown you wore. Yet in reality, very few brides are married in their mothers' dresses. Styles change quickly and most gowns don't appeal to brides of the future. Skip the gown preservation routine (and chemicals and costs associated with it) by donating your dress to charity. Brides Against Breast Cancer is a good choice—they resell your gown and donate the proceeds to benefit breast cancer patients and research.

Things to Consider: In selecting your formal wear, keep in mind the formality of your wedding, the time of day, and the bride's gown. Consider darker colors for a fall or winter wedding and lighter colors for a spring or summer wedding. When selecting a place to rent your tuxedo, check the reputation of the shop. Make sure they have a wide variety of makes and styles to choose from.

Reserve tuxedos for yourself and your ushers several weeks before the wedding to ensure a wide selection and to allow enough time for alterations. Plan to pick up the tuxedos a few days before the wedding to allow time for last-minute alterations in case they don't fit properly. Out-of-town men in your wedding party can be sized at any tuxedo shop. They can send their measurements to you or directly to the shop where you are going to rent your tuxedos.

Ask about the store's return policy and be sure you delegate to the appropriate person (usually your best man) the responsibility of returning all tuxedos within the time allotted. Ushers customarily pay for their own tuxedos.

Tips to Save Money: Try to negotiate getting your tuxedo for free or at a discount in exchange for having your father, your fiancé's father, and ushers rent their tuxedos at that shop.

Price Range: $60 - $200

BRIDAL ATTIRE CHECKLIST

ITEM	Description	Source
Full Slip		
Garter		
Gloves		
Gown		
Handbag		
Jewelry		
Lingerie		
Panty Hose		
Petticoat or Slip		
Shoes		
Something Old		
Something New		
Something Borrowed		
Something Blue		
Stocking		
Veil/Hat		
Other:		
Other:		
Other:		
Other:		

BRIDAL BOUTIQUE COMPARISON CHART

Questions	POSSIBILITY 1
What is the name of the bridal boutique?	
What is the website and e-mail of the bridal boutique?	
What is the address of the bridal boutique?	
What is the name and phone number of my contact person?	
What are your hours of operation? Are appointments needed?	
Do you offer any discounts or giveaways?	
What major bridal gown lines do you carry?	
Do you carry outfits for the mother of the bride?	
Do you carry bridesmaids gowns and/or tuxedos?	
Do you carry outfits for the flower girl and ring bearer?	
What is the cost of the desired bridal gown?	
What is the cost of the desired headpiece?	
Do you offer in-house alterations? If so, what are your fees?	
Do you carry bridal shoes? What is their price range?	
Do you dye shoes to match outfits?	
Do you rent bridal slips? If so, what is the rental fee?	
What is the estimated date of delivery for my gown?	
What is your payment policy/cancellation policy?	

POSSIBILITY 2	POSSIBILITY 3

BRIDAL ATTIRE

Bridal Boutique: _____

Date Ordered: _____

Salesperson: _____ Phone: _____

Address: _____

City: _____ State: _____ Zip: _____

Website: _____

E-mail: _____

Description of Dress: _____

	Manufacturer	Style	Size	Cost
Wedding Gown				
Headpiece				
Veil/Hat				
Shoes				

GOWN ALTERATIONS

Location: _____

Cost: _____

Tailor: _____ Phone: _____

Address: _____

City: _____ State: _____ Zip: _____

Website: _____

E-mail: _____

	Manufacturer	Style
First Alteration		
Second Alteration		
Third Alteration		
Final Alteration		

Bridal Boutique: _____

Date Ordered: _____

Salesperson: _____ Phone: _____

Address: _____

City: _____ State: _____ Zip: _____

Website: _____

E-mail: _____

Description of Dress: _____

Cost: _____

Manufacturer: _____

Date Ready: _____

BRIDESMAIDS' SIZES

Name	Dress	Height	Bust	Waist	Shoes

GROOM/GROOMSMEN'S ATTIRE

Store Name:

Date Ordered:

Salesperson: Phone:

Address:

City: State: Zip:

Website:

E-mail:

Description of Tuxedo:

Cost:

Manufacturer:

Date Ready:

GROOM/GROOMSMEN'S SIZES

Name	Height	Waist	Sleeve	Inseam	Jacket	Neck	Shoes

Photography

THE PHOTOGRAPHS TAKEN AT YOUR wedding are the best way to preserve your special day. Chances are you and your fiancé will look at the photos many times during your lifetime. Therefore, hiring a good photographer is one of the most important tasks in planning your wedding.

BRIDE & GROOM'S ALBUM

The bride and groom's photo album is the traditional way to preserve your special day. You and your spouse will look at the photos many times during your lifetime. Therefore, hiring a good photographer is one of the most important tasks in planning your wedding.

Options: There are a large variety of wedding albums. They vary in size, color, material, construction and price. Traditional-style albums frame each individual photo in a mat on the page. Digitally designed "Montage" albums group the photos in a creatively designed fashion for a more modern look.

Find one that you like and will feel proud of showing to your friends and family. Some of the most popular manufacturers of wedding albums are Art Leather, Leather Craftsman, Capri and Renaissance.

Keep in mind however, that the quality of the original photographs will determine how the finished album looks so choose your photographer for their skills, not necessarily the manufacturer of the album. Make sure you are shown the different styles of album available.

Different papers are available to print your photos, pearl and metallic as well as black and white can be chosen. Ask to see samples.

Things to Consider: Make sure you hire a photographer who specializes in weddings. Your photographer should be experienced in wedding procedures and familiar with your ceremony and reception sites. This will allow him/her to anticipate your next move and be in the proper place at the right time to capture all the special moments. Personal rapport is extremely important. The photographer may be an expert, but if you don't feel comfortable or at ease with him or her, your photography will reflect this. Comfort and compatibility with your photographer can make or break your wedding day and your photographs!

Look at his or her work. See if the photographer captured the excitement and emotion of the bridal couple. Also, remember that the wedding album should unfold like a story book -- the story of your wedding. Be sure to discuss with your photographer the photos you want so that there is no misunderstanding. A good wedding photographer will plan the day with you to ensure that all the important moments are covered. It is acceptable to take a list of important photos to your planning session before the wedding (even one copied from a wedding planning book). This will keep you on track and ensure that you've asked about all the photos that are "must haves."

Ask to look at albums that the photographer has ready to be delivered, or proofs of weddings recently photographed. Study the photographer's style. It's fine if they tell you that they're skilled in "photojournalistic" or "candid" photography but, if that's so, you should see plenty of candid-style shots in their portfolio! Some photographers are known for formal poses, while others specialize in more candid, creative shots. Some can do both.

When asked to provide references, photographers will obviously give you names of clients that they know are pleased with their work. (Why give a name of someone who wasn't?) So keep this in mind if you decide to call a former client.

When comparing prices, compare the quantity and size of the photographs in your album and the type of album that each photographer will use. Ask how many photos will be taken on average at a wedding of your size. Some photographers do not work with proofs. Rather, they simply supply you with a finished album after the wedding. Doing this may reduce the cost of your album but will also reduce your selection of photographs. Many photographers will put your proofs on a DVD for viewing. This is much less bulky and an easy way to preview all of your wedding photos.

Beware: Make sure the photographer you interview is the specific person that will photograph your wedding. Many companies have more than one photographer. The more professional companies will make sure that you meet with (and view the work of) THE photographer that will photograph your wedding. This way you can get an idea of his or her style and personality and begin to establish a rapport with YOUR photographer. Your chosen photographers name should go on your contract!

Also, some churches do not allow photographs to be shot during the ceremony. Please find out the rules and present them to your photographer so he is knowledgeable about your site.

Tips to Save Money: Consider hiring a professional photographer for the formal shots of your ceremony only. You can then place disposable cameras on each table at the reception and let your guests take candid shots. This will save you a considerable amount of money in photography.

You can also lower the price of your album by paying for the photographs and then putting them into the album yourself. This is a very time-consuming task, so your photographer may reduce the price of his or her package if you opt to do this. To really save money, select a photographer who charges a flat fee to shoot the wedding and allows you to purchase the film.

Compare at least three photographers for quality, value, and price. Photographers who shoot weddings "on the side" are usually less expensive, but the quality of their photographs may not be as good. Select less 8 x 10s for your album and more 4 x 6s, and choose a moderately priced album. Ask for specials and package deals.

Price Range: $900 - $9,000

ENGAGEMENT PHOTOGRAPH

Many couples are interested in a set of engagement photos to accompany their wedding-day photography. These make a nice keepsake for the couple, as well as a gift for friends and family. If taken far enough in advance, you can even include these photos in your Save the Date cards.

Things to Consider: Modernly, most couples prefer to have engagement photos taken outside and not in a studio. Ask your photographer if he or she can scout locations. Decide whether you want candid shots or posed portrait shots or a combination of both. On the day of the shoot, bring more than one wardrobe change and wear nice shoes, as many shots will be full-body. Engagement shoots usually include affectionate shots such as the couple hugging or even kissing, so talk to your partner about what you're both comfortable with. Finally, ask your photographer to take some classic bridal portraits (shots of just bride).

Tips to Save Money: Consider hiring the same photographer for engagement photos as for the wedding; many will build the price into the total photography package. To really cut costs, ask a friend or family member take photos of you and your fiancé.

Price Range: $75 - $300

FORMAL BRIDAL PORTRAIT

You may want a studio bridal portrait taken a few weeks before the wedding. Traditionally, this photo was sent to the newspaper to announce a marriage; however, few newspapers still accept these announcements.

Things to Consider: Some fine bridal salons provide an attractive background where the bride may arrange to have her formal bridal photograph taken after the final fitting of her gown. This will save you the hassle of bringing your gown and headpiece to the photographer's studio and dressing up once again.

Tips to Save Money: Consider having your formal portrait taken the day of your wedding. This will save you the studio costs and the hassle of getting dressed for the photo. The photograph will be more natural since the bridal bouquet will be the one you carry down the aisle. Also, brides are always most beautiful on their wedding day!

Price Range: $75 - $300

PARENTS' ALBUM

The parents' album is a smaller version of the bride and groom's album. It usually contains about twenty 5" x 7" photographs. Photos should be carefully selected for each individual family. If given as a gift, the album can be personalized with the bride and groom's names and date of their wedding on the front cover. Small "Coffee Table" books can also be created from digital files that are montaged onto the pages. Ask to see samples of different types of parent albums available.

Tips to Save Money: Try to negotiate at least one free parents' album with the purchase of the bride and groom's album.

Price Range: $100 - $600

PROOFS/PREVIEWS

Proofs/previews or Proof DVDs are the preliminary prints or digital images from which the bride and groom select photographs for their album and for their parents' albums. The prints vary from 4x5" to 5x5" and 4x6". The DVD allows you to view your photos on a screen in a larger size and more detail.

Things to Consider: When selecting a package, ask how many photos the photographer will take. The more images, the wider the selection you will have to choose from. For a wide selection, the photographer must take at least 3 to 5 times the number of prints that will go into your album.

Ask the photographer how soon after the wedding you will get your proofs. Request this in writing. Ideally, the proofs will be ready by the time you get back from your honeymoon.

Tips to Save Money: Ask your photographer to use your proofs as part of your album package to save developing costs.

Price Range: $100 - $600

DIGITAL FILES

Most digital files are presented as "Jpegs," which is the file type that most labs use to make prints. Your photographer will probably shoot with a professional digital camera that can create extra-large file sizes, which is important for clarity, if you want very large prints made (such as 24x30" and larger).

Things to Consider: Most photographers will not sell you the digital files up front since they hope to make a profit on selling extra prints after the wedding. Ask the photographers you interview how long they keep the files and at what point they will become available to you. A professional photographer should keep a backup copy of the digital files for at least 10 years.

Many photographers will sell you the entire set of digital files after all photos have been ordered by family and friends. Often the price will vary, depending on the amount spent on re-orders. Once you own your digital files, make a back-up copy of your disk every 5 or 6 years, as CDs and DVDs can deteriorate after 8 years or so.

Tips to Save Money: If you can wait, consider contacting the photographer a few years later and ask if he or she will sell you the files at that time. Most photographers will be glad to sell them at a bargain price.

Price Range: $100 - $800

EXTRA PRINTS

Extra prints are photographs ordered in addition to the main album or parents' albums. These are usually purchased as gifts for the bridal party, close friends and family members.

Things to Consider: It is important to discuss the cost of extra prints with your photographer since prices vary considerably. Knowing what extra prints will cost ahead of time will help you know if the photographer is truly within your budget. Think how many extra prints you would like to order and figure this into your budget before selecting a photographer.

Tips to Save Money: If you can wait, consider not ordering any reprints during the first few years after the wedding. A few years later, contact the photographer and ask if he or she will sell you the files. Most photographers will be glad to sell them at a bargain price at a later date. You can then make as many prints as you wish for a fraction of the cost.

Price Range: 5 x 7, $5 to $20; 8 x 10, $15 to $30; 11 x 14, $30 to $100

PHOTOGRAPHERS COMPARISON CHART

Questions	POSSIBILITY 1
What is the name and phone number of the photographer?	
What is the website and e-mail of the photographer?	
What is the address of the photographer?	
How many years of experience do you have as a photographer?	
What percentage of your business is dedicated to weddings?	
Approximately how many weddings have you photographed?	
Are you the person who will photograph my wedding?	
Will you bring an assistant with you to my wedding?	
How do you typically dress for weddings?	
Do you have a professional studio?	
What type of equipment do you use?	
Do you bring backup equipment with you to weddings?	
Do you need to visit the ceremony and reception sites prior to the wedding?	
Do you have liability insurance?	
Are you skilled in diffused lighting and soft focus?	
Can you take studio portraits?	
Can you retouch my images?	

POSSIBILITY 2	POSSIBILITY 3

PHOTOGRAPHERS COMPARISON CHART

Questions	POSSIBILITY 2
Can digital files be purchased? If so, what is the cost?	
What is the cost of the package I am interested in?	
What is your payment policy?	
What is your cancellation policy?	
Do you offer a money-back guarantee?	
Do you use paper proofs or DVD proofing?	
How many photographs will I have to choose from?	
When will I get my proofs?	
When will I get my album?	
What is the cost of an engagement portrait?	
What is the cost of a formal bridal portrait?	
What is the cost of a parent album?	
What is the cost of a 5 x 7 reprint?	
What is the cost of an 8 x 10 reprint?	
What is the cost of an 11 x 14 reprint?	
What is the cost per additional hour of shooting at the wedding?	

POSSIBILITY 2	POSSIBILITY 3

PHOTOGRAPHER'S INFORMATION SHEET

Once it is completed, make a copy of this form to give to your photographer as a reminder of your various events.

THE WEDDING OF : _____ Phone: _____

PHOTOGRAPHER'S COMPANY

Business Name: _____

Address: _____

City: _____ State: _____ Zip: _____

Website: _____ E-mail: _____

Photographer's Name: _____ Phone: _____

Assistant's Name: _____ Phone: _____

ENGAGEMENT PHOTOGRAPH

Date: _____ Time: _____

Location: _____

Address: _____

City: _____ State: _____ Zip: _____

BRIDAL PORTRAIT

Date: _____ Time: _____

Location: _____

Address: _____

City: _____ State: _____ Zip: _____

PHOTOGRAPHER'S INFORMATION SHEET

Once it is completed, make a copy of this form to give to your photographer as a reminder of your various events.

OTHER EVENTS

Event:

Date: Time:

Location:

Address:

City: State: Zip:

CEREMONY

Date: Arrival Time: Departure:

Location:

Address:

City: State: Zip:

Ceremony Restrictions/Guidelines:

RECEPTION

Date: Arrival Time: Departure:

Time:

Location:

Address:

City: State: Zip:

Reception Restrictions/Guidelines:

WEDDING PHOTOGRAPHS

Check off all photographs you would like taken throughout your wedding day.
Then make a copy of this form and give it to your photographer.

PRE-CEREMONY PHOTOGRAPHS

- ❑ Bride leaving her house
- ❑ Wedding rings with the invitation
- ❑ Bride getting dressed for the ceremony
- ❑ Bride looking at her bridal bouquet
- ❑ Maid of honor putting garter on bride's leg
- ❑ Bride by herself
- ❑ Bride with her mother
- ❑ Bride with her father
- ❑ Bride with mother and father
- ❑ Bride with her entire family and/or any combination thereof
- ❑ Bride with her maid of honor
- ❑ Bride with her bridesmaids
- ❑ Bride with the flower girl and/or ring bearer
- ❑ Bride's mother putting on her corsage
- ❑ Groom leaving his house
- ❑ Groom putting on his boutonniere
- ❑ Groom with his mother
- ❑ Groom with his father
- ❑ Groom with mother and father
- ❑ Groom with his entire family and/or any combination thereof
- ❑ Groom with his best man
- ❑ Groom with his ushers
- ❑ Groom shaking hands with his best man while looking at his watch
- ❑ Groom with the bride's father
- ❑ Bride and her father getting out of the limousine
- ❑ Special members of the family being seated
- ❑ Groom waiting for the bride before the processional
- ❑ Bride and her father just before the processional

Check off all photographs you would like taken throughout your wedding day.
Then make a copy of this form and give it to your photographer.

OTHER PRE-CEREMONY PHOTOGRAPHS YOU WOULD LIKE

❏ _____

❏ _____

❏ _____

CEREMONY PHOTOGRAPHS

❏ The processional
❏ Bride and groom saying their vows
❏ Bride and groom exchanging rings
❏ Groom kissing the bride at the altar
❏ The recessional

OTHER CEREMONY PHOTOS YOU WOULD LIKE

❏ _____

❏ _____

❏ _____

POST-CEREMONY PHOTOGRAPHS

❏ Bride and groom
❏ Newlyweds with both of their families
❏ Newlyweds with the entire wedding party
❏ Bride and groom signing the marriage certificate
❏ Flowers and other decorations

OTHER POST-CEREMONY PHOTOS YOU WOULD LIKE

❏ _____

❏ _____

❏ _____

WEDDING PHOTOGRAPHS

Check off all photographs you would like taken throughout your wedding day.
Then make a copy of this form and give it to your photographer.

RECEPTION PHOTOGRAPHS

- ❏ Entrance of newlyweds and wedding party into the reception site
- ❏ Receiving line
- ❏ Guests signing the guest book
- ❏ Toasts
- ❏ First dance
- ❏ Bride and her father dancing
- ❏ Groom and his mother dancing
- ❏ Bride dancing with groom's father
- ❏ Groom dancing with bride's mother
- ❏ Wedding party and guests dancing
- ❏ Cake tables
- ❏ Cake-cutting ceremony
- ❏ Couple feeding each other cake
- ❏ Buffet table and its decoration
- ❏ Bouquet-tossing ceremony
- ❏ Garter-tossing ceremony
- ❏ Musicians
- ❏ The wedding party table
- ❏ The family tables
- ❏ Candid shots of your guests
- ❏ Bride and groom saying goodbye to their parents
- ❏ Bride and groom looking back, waving goodbye in the getaway car

OTHER RECEPTION PHOTOS YOU WOULD LIKE

- ❏ _____
- ❏ _____
- ❏ _____
- ❏ _____
- ❏ _____
- ❏ _____

Videography

NEXT TO YOUR PHOTO ALBUM,
videography is the best way to
preserve your wedding memories.
Unlike photographs, videography
captures the mood of the wedding
day in motion and sound.

Getting a wedding on video used to mean bright lights, cables, microphones and huge obtrusive cameras. But technology has changed, and today's videographers have more advanced equipment that allows them to film ceremonies with minimal disruption.

Today's wedding videos can also be edited and professionally produced, with music, slow motion, black and white scenes and many other special features. You have the option of selecting one, two, or three cameras to record your wedding. The more cameras used, the more action your videographer can capture—and the more expensive the service. An experienced videographer,

however, can do a good job with just one camera.

Options: There are two basic types of wedding video production: documentary and cinematic. The documentary type production records your wedding day as it happened, in real time. Very little editing or embellishment is involved. These types of videos are normally less expensive and can be delivered within days after the wedding.

The cinematic type production is more reminiscent of a movie. Although it can be shot with one camera, most good cinematic wedding videos are shot with two cameras, allowing one videographer to focus on the events as they happen while the other gathers footage that will be added later to enhance the final result. This type of video requires more time due to the extensive editing of the footage, which can take up to 40 hours of studio time.

You may wish to have both of these—one straightforward version and another version with all the details and a nice, theatrical flow.

The latest technology includes the option of producing video in high definition. More televisions are being manufactured with high definition resolution, which delivers a much sharper picture than traditional sets. In years to come, viewers will encounter problems watching regular DVDs on their hi-def television sets. Standard definition video appears fuzzy and pixilated on the new high definition monitors. Having your ceremony shot in high definition will ensure that you'll be able to enjoy watching your wedding video in a crisp, clear resolution for years to come.

MAIN VIDEO

You will need to choose the type of video you want. Do you want the footage edited down to a 30-minute film, or do you want an "as it happened" replay? Remember, an edited video will require more time and will therefore be more expensive than just a documentary of the events.

GREEN WEDDING TIP

Get a Green Videographer
Like green photographers, a green videographer will employ the principles of reduce, reuse, and recycle in every aspect of his or her business. A green videographer will recycle the materials related to their work, drive to jobs in an environmentally responsible vehicle, and conserve resources in their workspace. Plus, having your wedding digitally videotaped allows you to keep the guest list small. You can then send copies of the ceremony to friends and family you weren't able to invite due to the high environmental cost of their travel.

Things to Consider: Be sure to hire a videographer who specializes in weddings and ask to see samples of his or her work. Weddings are very specialized events. A $1,000 video camera in the hands of a seasoned professional "wedding" videographer will produce far better results than a $3,000 broadcast quality camera or a $4,000 high definition camera in the hands of just an average camera operator. When considering a particular videographer, look at previous weddings the videographer has done. Notice the color and brightness of the screen, as well as the quality of sound. This will indicate the quality of his or her equipment. Note whether the picture is smooth or jerky. This will indicate the videographer's skill level. Ask about special effects such as titles, dissolve, and multiple screens. Find out what's included in the cost of your package so that there are no surprises at the end!

If you will be getting married in a church, find out the church's policies regarding videography. Some churches might require the videographer to film the ceremony from a specific distance.

Beware: As in photography, there are many companies with more than one videographer. These companies may use the work of their best videographer to sell their packages and then send a less experienced videographer to the wedding. Again, don't get caught in this trap! Be sure to interview the videographer who will shoot your wedding so you can get a good idea of his or her style and personality. Ask to see his or her own work.

Tips to Save Money: Compare videographers' quality, value, and price. There is a wide range, and the most expensive is not necessarily the best. The videographer who uses one camera (instead of multiple cameras) is usually the most cost effective and may be all you need.

Consider hiring a company that offers both videography and photography. You might save money by combining the two services.

Ask a family member or close friend to videotape your wedding. However, realize that without professional equipment and expertise, the final product may not be quite as polished.

Price Range: $600 - $4,000

TITLES

Titles and subtitles can be edited into your video before or after the filming. Titles are important since twenty years from now you might not remember the exact time of your wedding or the names of your bridal party members. Some videographers charge more for titling. Make sure you discuss this with your videographer and get in writing exactly what titles will be included.

Options: Titles can include the date, time, and location of the wedding, the bride and groom's names, and the names of special members of the family and bridal party. Titles may also include special thanks to those who helped with the wedding. You can then send these people copies of your video, which would be a very appropriate and inexpensive gift!

Tips to Save Money: Consider asking for limited titles, such as only the names of the bride and groom and the date and time of the wedding.

Price Range: $50 - $300

EXTRA HOURS

Find out how much your videographer would charge to stay longer than the contracted time. Do this in case your reception lasts longer than expected. Don't forget to get this fee in writing.

Tips to Save Money: To avoid paying for hours beyond what's included in your selected package, calculate the maximum number of hours you think you'll need and negotiate that number of hours into your package price.

To reduce the amount of time you'll need to use the videographer, consider recording the ceremony only.

Price Range: $35 - $150 per hour

PHOTO MONTAGE

A photo montage is a series of photographs set to music on video. The number of photographs in your photo montage depends on the length of the songs and the amount of time allotted for each photograph. A typical song usually allows for thirty to forty photographs. Photo montages are a great way to display and reproduce your photographs. Copies of this video can be made for considerably less than the cost of reproducing photos.

Options: Your photo montage can include photos of you and your fiancé growing up in addition to shots from your rehearsal, wedding day, honeymoon, or any combination thereof.

Things to Consider: Send copies of your photo montage video to close friends and family members as mementos of your wedding.

Tips to Save Money: There are many websites on the Internet that allow you to create your own photo montage either for free or at a very low price. You can then transfer your photo montage to a DVD.

Price Range: $60 - $300

EXTRA COPIES

A videographer can produce higher quality copies than you can. Ask your videographer what the charge is for extra copies.

Tips to Save Money: If you have a digital video recorder, you can make copies of your wedding video using a second DVD player. It's easier, however, to burn DVDs on your computer. Before making your own copies of your wedding video, be sure to ask your videographer if that is acceptable. Many contracts prohibit it, and doing so could be copyright infringement. Further, your videographer may have put a security device on the DVD that would prevent you from being able to copy it.

Price Range: $15 - $50

VIDEOGRAPHY COMPARISON CHART

Questions	POSSIBILITY 1
What is the name and phone number of the videographer?	
What is the website and e-mail address of the videographer?	
What is the address of the videographer?	
How many years of experience do you have as a videographer?	
Approximately how many weddings have you videotaped?	
Are you the person who will videotape my wedding?	
Will you bring an assistant with you to my wedding?	
What type of equipment do you use?	
Do you have a wireless microphone?	
Do you bring backup equipment with you?	
Do you visit the ceremony and reception sites before the wedding?	
Do you edit the tape after the event?	
Who keeps the raw footage and for how long?	
When will I receive the final product?	
What is the cost of the desired package?	
What does it include?	
Can you make a photo montage?	
If so, what is your price?	
What is your payment policy?	
What is your cancellation policy?	

POSSIBILITY 2	POSSIBILITY 3

WEDDING PLANNING NOTES

Stationery

BEGIN CREATING YOUR GUEST LIST AS SOON as possible. Ask your parents and the groom's parents for a list of people they would like to invite. You and your fiancé should make your own lists. Make certain that all names are spelled correctly and that all addresses are current.

Determine if you wish to include children; if so, add their names to your list. All children over the age of 16 should receive their own invitation.

INVITATIONS

Order your invitations at least four months before the wedding. Allow an additional month for engraved invitations. Invitations are traditionally issued by the bride's parents; but if the groom's parents are assuming some of the wedding expenses, the invitations should be in their names also. Mail all invitations at the same time, six to eight weeks before the wedding.

Options: There are three main types of invitations: traditional / formal, contemporary, and informal. The traditional / formal wedding invitation is white, soft cream, or ivory with raised black lettering. The printing is done on the top page of a double sheet of thick quality paper; the inside is left blank. The contemporary invitation is typically an individualized presentation that makes a statement about the bride and groom.

Informal invitations are often printed on the front of a single, heavyweight

What Is Eco-Friendly Stationery?
A lot of companies claim to make eco-friendly stationery. Know that truly green paper is made from at least 30 percent post-consumer content (i.e., recycled materials), but preferably 70 or 100 percent. It is often handmade and produced without acids or chlorine. It can come from a wood alternative, such as hemp. Environmentally friendly paper might be certified by the Forest Stewardship Council (FSC). Using one ton of 100 percent recycled paper saves 7,000 gallons of water, 17 trees, and enough energy to power a home for six months.

card and may be handwritten or preprinted. There are three types of printing: engraved, thermography, and offset printing. Engraving is the most expensive, traditional, and formal type of printing. It also takes the longest to complete. In engraved printing, stationery is pressed onto a copper plate, which makes the letters rise slightly from the page. Thermography is a process that fuses powder and ink to create a raised letter. This takes less time than engraving and is less expensive because copper plates do not have to be engraved. Offset printing, the least expensive, is the quickest to produce and offers a variety of styles and colors. It is also the least formal.

Things to Consider: If all your guests are to be invited to both the ceremony and the reception, a combined invitation may be sent without separate enclosure cards. Order one invitation for each married or cohabiting couple that you plan to invite. The officiant and his or her spouse, as well as your attendants, should receive an invitation.

Order approximately 20 percent more stationery than your actual count. Allow a minimum of two weeks to address and mail the invitations, longer if using a calligrapher or if your guest list is very large. You may also want to consider ordering invitations to the rehearsal dinner, as these should be in the same style as the wedding invitation.

SAMPLES OF TRADITIONAL/FORMAL INVITATIONS

1) When the bride's parents sponsor the wedding:

Mr. and Mrs. Alexander Waterman Smith
request the honor of your presence
at the marriage of their daughter

Carol Ann

to

Mr. William James Clark

on Saturday, the fifth of August

two thousand eight

at two o'clock in the afternoon

Saint James by-the-Sea

La Jolla, California

2) When the groom's parents sponsor the wedding:

Mr. and Mrs. Michael Burdell Clark

request the honor of your presence

at the marriage of

Miss Carol Ann Smith

to their son

Mr. William James Clark

3) When both the bride and groom's parents sponsor the wedding:

Mr. and Mrs. Alexander Waterman Smith

and

Mr. and Mrs. Michael Burdell Clark

request the honor of your presence

at the marriage of their children

Miss Carol Ann Smith

to

Mr. William James Clark

OR

Mr. and Mrs. Alexander Waterman Smith

request the honor of your presence

at the marriage of their daughter

Carol Ann Smith

to

William James Clark

son of Mr. and Mrs. Michael Burdell Clark

4) When the bride and groom sponsor their own wedding:

The honor of your presence is requested
at the marriage of
Miss Carol Ann Smith
and
Mr. William James Clark

OR

Miss Carol Ann Smith
and
Mr. William James Clark
request the honor of your presence
at their marriage

5) With divorced or deceased parents:

a) When the bride's mother is sponsoring the wedding and is not remarried:

Mrs. Julie Hurden Smith
requests the honor of your presence
at the marriage of her daughter
Carol Ann

b) When the bride's mother is sponsoring the wedding and has remarried:

Mrs. Julie Hurden Booker
requests the honor of your presence
at the marriage of her daughter
Carol Ann Smith

OR

Mr. and Mrs. John Thomas Booker
request the honor of your presence
at the marriage of Mrs. Booker's daughter
Carol Ann Smith

c) When the bride's father is sponsoring the wedding and has not remarried:

Mr. Alexander Waterman Smith
requests the honor of your presence
at the marriage of his daughter
Carol Ann

d) When the bride's father is sponsoring the wedding and has remarried:

Mr. and Mrs. Alexander Waterman Smith
request the honor of your presence
at the marriage of Mr. Smith's daughter
Carol Ann

6) With deceased parents:

a) When a close friend or relative sponsors the wedding:

Mr. and Mrs. Brandt Elliott Lawson
request the honor of your presence
at the marriage of their granddaughter
Carol Ann Smith

7) In military ceremonies, the rank
determines the placement of names:

**a) Any title lower than sergeant should be
omitted. Only the branch of service should
be included under that person's name:**

Mr. and Mrs. Alexander Waterman Smith
request the honor of your presence
at the marriage of their daughter
Carol Ann
to
William James Clark
United States Army

GREEN WEDDING TIP

Avoid Invitation Bling Traditional wedding invitations are often dressed up in a festive but wasteful presentation of decorative tissue, ribbons, raffia, fake flowers, beads, glitter, and other elements. When choosing your invitations, skip this kind of bling, and also avoid invitations that feature multiple pieces of paper stacked on top of each other. Doing so can save approximately 24 trees per each ton of paper, and will also cut down on the amount of waste sent to a landfill and carbon dioxide that is spewed into the atmosphere.

b) Junior officers' titles are placed below their names and are followed by their branch of service:

Mr. and Mrs. Alexander Waterman Smith
request the honor of your presence
at the marriage of their daughter
Carol Ann
to
William James Clark
First Lieutenant, United States Army

c) If the rank is higher than lieutenant, titles are placed before names, and the branch of service is placed on the following line:

Mr. and Mrs. Alexander Waterman Smith
request the honor of your presence
at the marriage of their daughter
Carol Ann
to
Captain William James Clark
United States Navy

SAMPLE OF A LESS FORMAL/MORE CONTEMPORARY INVITATION

Mr. and Mrs. Alexander Waterman Smith
would like you to
join with their daughter
Carol Ann
and
William James Clark
in the celebration of their marriage

For additional wording suggestions, log on to www.WedSpace.com

Tips to Save Money: Thermography looks like engraving and is one-third the cost. Choose paper stock that is reasonable and yet achieves your overall look. Select invitations that can be mailed using just one stamp. Order at least 25 extra invitations in case you soil some or add people to your list. To reorder this small number of invitations later would cost nearly three times the amount you'll spend up front.

Price Range: $0.75 - $6 per invitation

RESPONSE CARDS

Response cards are enclosed with the invitation to determine the number of people who will be attending your wedding. They are the smallest card size accepted by the postal service and should be printed in the same style as the invitation. An invitation to only the wedding ceremony does not usually include a request for a reply. However, response cards should be used when it is necessary to have an exact head count for special seating arrangements. Response cards are widely accepted today. If included, these cards should be easy for your guests to understand and use. Include a self-addressed and stamped return envelope to make it easy for your guests to return the response cards.

Things to Consider: You should not include a line that reads "number of persons" on your response cards because only those whose names appear on the inner and outer envelopes are invited. Each couple, each single person, and all children over the age of 16 should receive their own invitation. Indicate on the inner envelope if they may bring an escort or guest. The omitting of children's names from the inner envelope infers that the children are not invited.

Samples of wording for response cards:

M_____

(The M may be eliminated from the line, especially if many Drs. are invited)

GREEN WEDDING TIP

View the Envelope as Enemy In addition to being another piece of paper to waste, envelopes often contain glue made from toxic materials that harm the environment in their creation. Aim to use as few envelopes as possible. Send save-the-date and thank you notes as postcards or magnets. Also use postcards for RSVP cards (or go a step further and offer an email address where guests can send their response). Some companies print addresses directly on the back of your invitation, eliminating the need for an envelope entirely.

GREEN WEDDING TIP

Plant Your Stationery For unique and elegant stationery, choose seed-embedded paper. This handmade, recycled paper is embedded with wildflower seeds. The invitation is torn up, planted in a pot or garden, and leaves behind nothing but festive blooms. An innovator in this stationery is Green Field Paper Company. In addition to flower seed-embedded paper, Green Field offers invites made from recycled junk mail and paper infused with garlic skins or roasted coffee. Another company, Diva Entertains, offers plantable invitations, place cards, favors, and other products.

___ accepts

___ regrets

Saturday the fifth of July

Oceanside Country Club

OR

The favor of your reply is requested
by the twenty-second of May

M_____

will _____ attend

Price Range: $0.40 - $1 each

RECEPTION CARDS

If the guest list for the ceremony is larger than that for the reception, a separate card with the date, time and location for the reception should be enclosed with the ceremony invitation for those guests also invited to the reception. Reception cards should be placed in front of the invitation, facing the back flap and the person inserting them. They should be printed on the same quality paper and in the same style as the invitation itself.

Sample of a formally worded reception card:

Mr. and Mrs. Alexander Waterman Smith
request the pleasure of your company

GREEN WEDDING TIP

Look Behind the Envelope A lot of companies sell eco-friendly stationery, but not all are authentic. You will have found a truly green paper provider when the operation is a privately owned shop that gives a portion of its profits to charity. Some of its electricity will come from green sources such as hydro or solar power. Water used to make paper will be partially recycled, and they won't send bulky catalogues or drown you in samples. Their products will be printed on a digital press that emits no Volatile Organic Compounds (VOCs).

Saturday, the third of July
at three o'clock
Oceanside Country Club
2020 Waterview Lane
Oceanside, California

Sample of a less formal reception card:
Reception immediately following the ceremony
Oceanside Country Club
2020 Waterview Lane
Oceanside, California

Things to Consider: You may also include a reception card in all your invitations if the reception is to be held at a different site than the ceremony.

Tips to Save Money: If all people invited to the ceremony are also invited to the reception, include the reception information on the invitation and eliminate the reception card. This will save printing and postage costs.

Price Range: $0.40 - $1 each

CEREMONY CARDS

If the guest list for the reception is larger than the guest list for the ceremony, a special insertion card with the date, time, and location for the ceremony should be enclosed with the reception invitation for those guests also invited to the ceremony.

Ceremony cards should be placed in front of the invitation, facing the back flap and the person inserting them. They should be printed on the same quality paper and in the same style as the invitation itself.

Price Range: $0.40 - $1 each

 GREEN WEDDING TIP

Use Paper Alternatives Investigate stationery made from a paper alternative—you will be amazed at what materials some companies work with! Popular options include bamboo, hemp, banana stalks, cotton, elephant dung, flax, hemp, cloth, petals, flowers, silk, and grass. In addition to being handmade, acid- and chlorine-free, and made from recycled products, many of these materials won't disintegrate or discolor with time, as wood pulp-based paper often does. Only your budget will limit your choice of the many paper alternatives on the market today.

PEW CARDS

Pew cards may be used to let special guests and family members know they are to be seated in the reserved section on either the bride's side or the groom's side. These are typically seen in formal ceremonies. Guests should take this card to the ceremony and show it to the ushers, who should then escort them to their seats.

Options: Pew cards may indicate a specific pew number if specific seats are assigned, or may read "Within the Ribbon" if pews are reserved, but no specific seat is assigned.

Things to Consider: These may inserted along with the invitation, or may be sent separately after the RSVPs have been returned. It is easier to send them after you have received all RSVPs so you know how many reserved pews will be needed.

Tips to Save Money: Include the pew card with the invitation to special guests and just say, "Within the Ribbon." After you have received all your RSVPs, you will know how many pews need to be reserved. This will save you the cost of mailing the pew cards separately.

Price Range: $0.25 - $1 each

SEATING/PLACE CARDS

Seating/place cards are used to let guests know where they should be seated at the reception and are a good way of putting people together so they feel most comfortable. Place cards should be laid out alphabetically on a table at the entrance to the reception. Each card should correspond to a table—either by number, color, or other identifying factor. Each table should be marked accordingly.

Options: Select a traditional or contemporary design for your place cards, depending on the style of your wedding. Regardless of the design, place cards must contain the same information: the bride and groom's names on the first line; the date on the second line; the third line is left blank for you to write in the guest's name; and the fourth line is for the table number, color, or other identifying factor.

Price Range: $0.25 - $1 each

RAIN CARDS

These cards are enclosed when guests are invited to an outdoor ceremony and/or reception, informing them of an alternate location in case of bad weather. As with other enclosures, rain cards should be placed in front of the invitation, facing the back flap and the person inserting them. They should be printed on the same quality paper and in the same style as the invitation itself.

Price Range: $0.25 - $1 each

MAPS

Maps to the ceremony and/or reception are becoming frequent inserts in wedding invitations. They need to be drawn and printed in the same style as the invitation and are usually on a small, heavier card. If they are not printed in the same style or on the same type of paper as the invitation, they should be mailed separately.

Options: Maps should include both written and visual instructions, keeping in mind the fact that guests may be coming from different locations.

Things to Consider: Order extra maps to hand out at the ceremony if the reception is at a different location.

 GREEN WEDDING TIP

Go Paperless In 2008, *The San Francisco Chronicle* reported that the average cost of paper wedding invitations was $943. When you add postage to the mix, the cost of sending paper is well over a thousand bucks. Many couples are opting to save this money, and the resulting paper waste, by using electronic wedding invitations. Several companies offer e-wedding invitations that retain a sense of formality and propriety. For example, Greenvelope is one company that sends formal, individual digital invitations to each of your guests.

Tips to Save Money: If you are comfortable with computers, you can purchase software that allows you to draw your own maps. Print a map to both the ceremony and reception on the same sheet of paper, perhaps one on each side. This will save you the cost of mailing two maps. Or have your ushers hand out maps to the reception after the ceremony.

Price Range: $0.50 - $1 each

CEREMONY PROGRAMS

Ceremony programs are printed documents showing the sequence of events during the ceremony. These programs add a personal touch to your wedding and are a convenient way of letting guests know who your attendants, officiant, and ceremony musicians are.

Options: Ceremony programs can be handed out by the ushers, or they can be placed at the back of the church for guests to take as they enter.

Price Range: $0.75 - $3 each

ANNOUNCEMENTS

Announcements are not obligatory but serve a useful purpose. They may be sent to friends who are not invited to the wedding because the number of guests must be limited or because they live too far away. They may also be sent to acquaintances who, while not particularly close to the family, might still wish to know about the marriage.

Announcements are also appropriate for friends and acquaintances who are not expected to attend and for whom you do not want to give an obligation of sending a gift. They should include the day, month, year, city, and state where the ceremony took place.

Things to Consider: Announcements should never be sent to anyone who has received an invitation to the ceremony or the reception. They are printed on the same paper and in the same style as the invitation. They should be addressed before the wedding and mailed the day of or the day after the ceremony.

Price Range: $0.75 - $2 each

THANK-YOU NOTES

Regardless of whether the bride has thanked the donor in person or not, she must write a thank-you note for every gift received.

Things to Consider: Order thank-you notes along with your other stationery at least four months before your wedding. You should order some with your maiden initials for thank-you notes sent before the ceremony, and the rest with your married initials for notes sent after the wedding and for future use. Send thank-you notes within two weeks of receiving a gift that arrives before the wedding, and within two months after the honeymoon for gifts received on or after your wedding day. Be sure to mention the gift you received in the body of the note and let the person know how much you like it and what you plan to do with it.

Price Range: $0.40 - $0.75 each

STAMPS

Don't forget to budget stamps for response cards as well as for invitations!

Things to Consider: Don't order stamps until you have had the post office weigh your completed invitation. It may exceed the size and weight for one stamp. Order commemorative stamps that fit the occasion.

Price Range: $0.39 - $1 each

 GREEN WEDDING TIP

Use E-invites Only When Appropriate For formal and large weddings, it remains appropriate to send a hard copy of an invitation. E-invitations can alienate older guests who are uncomfortable using the computer or who want the keepsake of an invitation. Secondly, the casual nature of e-invites is such that people can forget to respond to them. In these cases, reserve e-invitations for less formal announcements. E-stationery is also good for festivities surrounding the wedding, such as the rehearsal dinner, bridal shower, and bachelorette and bachelor parties.

CALLIGRAPHY

Calligraphy is a form of elegant handwriting often used to address invitations for formal occasions. Traditional wedding invitations should be addressed in black or blue fountain pen.

Options: You may address the invitations yourself, hire a professional calligrapher, or have your invitations addressed using calligraphy by computer. Make sure you use the same method or person to address both the inner and outer envelopes.

Tips to Save Money: You may want to consider taking a short course to learn the art of calligraphy so that you can address your own invitations. If you have a computer with a laser printer, you can address the invitations yourself using one of many beautiful calligraphy fonts.

Price Range: $0.50 - $3 each

NAPKINS/MATCHBOOKS

Napkins and matchbooks may also be ordered from your stationer. These are placed around the reception room as decorative items and mementos of the event.

Things to Consider: Napkins and matchbooks can be printed in your wedding colors, or simply white with gold or silver lettering. Include both of your names and the wedding date. You may consider including a phrase or thought, or a small graphic design above your names.

Price Range: $0.50 - $1.50 each

STATIONERY ITEM	Qty	Cost
❑ Invitations		
❑ Envelopes		
❑ Response Cards/Envelopes		
❑ Reception Cards		
❑ Ceremony Cards		
❑ Pew Cards		
❑ Seating/Place Cards		
❑ Rain Cards		
❑ Maps		
❑ Ceremony Programs		
❑ Announcements		
❑ Thank-You Notes		
❑ Stamps		
❑ Personalized Napkins/Matchbooks		
❑ Other:		
❑ Other:		
❑ Other:		

The Marriage of
Carol Ann Smith and William James Clark
the eleventh of March, 2008
San Diego, California

OUR CEREMONY

Prelude:
All I Ask of You, by Andrew Lloyd Webber

Processional:
Canon in D Major, by Pachelbel

Rite of Marriage

Welcome guests

Statement of intentions

Marriage vows

Exchange of rings

Blessing of bride and groom

Pronouncement of marriage

Presentation of the bride and groom

Recessional:
Trumpet Voluntary, by Jeromiah Clarke

OUR WEDDING PARTY

Maid of Honor:
Susan Smith, Sister of Bride

Best Man:
Brandt Clark, Brother of Groom

Bridesmaids:
Janet Anderson, Friend of Bride
Lisa Bennett, Friend of Bride

Ushers:
Mark Gleason, Friend of Groom
Tommy Olson, Friend of Groom

Officiant:
Father Henry Thomas

OUR RECEPTION

Please join us after the ceremony
in the celebration of our marriage at:
La Valencia Hotel
1132 Prospect Street
La Jolla, California

STATIONERY COMPARISON CHART

Questions	POSSIBILITY 1
What is the name and phone number of the stationery provider?	
What is the website and e-mail of the stationery provider?	
What is the address of the stationery provider?	
How many years of experience do you have?	
What lines of stationery do you carry?	
What types of printing processes do you offer?	
How soon in advance does the order have to be placed?	
What is the turnaround time?	
What is the cost of the desired invitation? Announcement?	
What is the cost of the desired response card? Reception card?	
What is the cost of the desired thank-you note?	
What is the cost of the desired party favors?	
What is the cost of the desired wedding program?	
What is the cost of addressing the envelopes in calligraphy?	
What is your payment policy?	
What is your cancellation policy?	

POSSIBILITY 2	POSSIBILITY 3

STATIONERY INFORMATION

Stationer: _____

Date Ordered: _____

Salesperson: _____

Phone: _____

Address: _____

City: _____ State: _____ Zip: _____

Website: _____

E-mail: _____

Stationery Item: (Include selections for Paper, Style, Color, Font, Printing)

Invitations/Envelopes: _____

Response Cards/Envelopes: _____

Reception Cards: _____

Ceremony Cards: _____

Pew Cards: _____

Seating/Place Cards: _____

Rain Cards: _____

Maps: _____

Ceremony Programs: _____

Announcements: _____

Thank-You Notes: _____

Napkins: _____

Matchbooks: _____

Invitations: _____
_____
_____
_____
_____
_____
_____

Announcements: _____
_____
_____
_____
_____

Reception Cards: _____
_____
_____

Response Cards: _____
_____
_____

Seating/Place Cards: _____
_____
_____

Napkins/Matchbooks: _____
_____
_____

GUEST & GIFT LIST

Make as many copies of this form as needed.

Name:

Address:

City: _____ State: _____ Zip: _____

Phone:

Email:

Table/Pew #:

Shower Gift: _____ ❑ Thank-You Note Sent

Wedding Gift: _____ ❑ Thank-You Note Sent

Name:

Address:

City: _____ State: _____ Zip: _____

Phone:

Email:

Table/Pew #:

Shower Gift: _____ ❑ Thank-You Note Sent

Wedding Gift: _____ ❑ Thank-You Note Sent

Name:

Address:

City: _____ State: _____ Zip: _____

Phone:

Email:

Table/Pew #:

Shower Gift: _____ ❑ Thank-You Note Sent

Wedding Gift: _____ ❑ Thank-You Note Sent

Make as many copies of this form as needed.

Name: _____

Address: _____

City: _____ State: _____ Zip: _____

Phone: _____

Email: _____

Name: _____

Address: _____

City: _____ State: _____ Zip: _____

Phone: _____

Email: _____

Name: _____

Address: _____

City: _____ State: _____ Zip: _____

Phone: _____

Email: _____

Name: _____

Address: _____

City: _____ State: _____ Zip: _____

Phone: _____

Email: _____

Name: _____

Address: _____

City: _____ State: _____ Zip: _____

Phone: _____

Email: _____

GUEST ACCOMMODATION LIST

*Make as many copies of this form as needed
to accommodate the size of your guest list.*

Name: _____

Arrival Date: _____ Time: _____

Airline: _____ Flight No.: _____

Pick Up By: _____

Will Stay At: _____

Phone: _____

Cost Per Room: _____ Confirmation No.: _____

Departure Date: _____ Time: _____

Taken By: _____

Airline: _____

Flight No.: _____

Name: _____

Arrival Date: _____ Time: _____

Airline: _____ Flight No.: _____

Pick Up By: _____

Will Stay At: _____

Phone: _____

Cost Per Room: _____ Confirmation No.: _____

Departure Date: _____ Time: _____

Taken By: _____

Airline: _____

Flight No.: _____

Addressing Invitations

WE RECOMMEND YOU START ADDRESSING your invitations at least three months before your wedding, and preferably four months if you are using calligraphy or if your guest list is above 200. You may want to ask your maid of honor or bridesmaids to help you with this time-consuming task, as this is traditionally part of their responsibilities.

Organize a luncheon or late afternoon get together with hors d'oeuvres and make a party out of it! If you are working with a wedding consultant, he or she can also help you address invitations.

There are typically two envelopes that need to be addressed for wedding invitations: an inner envelope and an outer envelope. The inner envelope is placed unsealed inside the outer envelope, with the flap away from the person inserting.

The invitation and all enclosures are placed inside the inner envelope facing the back flap. The inner envelope contains the name (or names) of the person (or people) who are invited to the ceremony and/or reception. The address is not included on the inner envelope.

The outer envelope contains the name (or names) and address of the person (or people) to whom the inner envelope belongs.

Use the guidelines on the following page to help you properly address both the inner and outer envelopes.

GUIDELINES FOR ADDRESSING INVITATIONS

Note: Inner envelope does not include first names or addresses.
The outer envelope includes first names and addresses.

Husband and Wife (with same surname)
Inner Envelope: Mr. and Mrs. Smith
Outer Envelope: Mr. and Mrs. Thomas Smith (use middle name, if known)

Husband and Wife (with different surnames)
Inner Envelope: Ms. Banks and Mr. Smith
                   (wife first)
Outer Envelope: Ms. Anita Banks
                   Mr. Thomas Smith (wife's name & title above husband's)

Husband and Wife (wife has professional title)
Inner Envelope: Dr. Smith and Mr. Smith (wife first)
Outer Envelope: Dr. Anita Smith Mr. Thomas Smith
                   (wife's name & title above husband's)

Husband and Wife (with children under 16)
Inner Envelope: Mr. and Mrs. Smith
                   John, Mary, and Glen (in order of age)
Outer Envelope: Mr. and Mrs. Thomas Smith

Single Woman (regardless of age)
Inner Envelope: Miss/Ms. Smith
Outer Envelope: Miss/Ms. Beverly Smith

Single Woman and Guest
Inner Envelope: Miss/Ms. Smith
                   Mr. Jones (or "and Guest")
Outer Envelope: Miss/Ms. Beverly Smith

Single Man
Inner Envelope: Mr. Jones (Master for a young boy)
Outer Envelope: Mr. William Jones

GUIDELINES FOR ADDRESSING INVITATIONS

Note: Inner envelope does not include first names or addresses.
The outer envelope includes first names and addresses.

Single Man and Guest
Inner Envelope: Mr. Jones
                          Miss/Ms. Smith (or "and Guest")
Outer Envelope: Mr. William Jones

Unmarried Couple Living Together
Inner Envelope: Mr. Knight and Ms. Orlandi
                          (names listed alphabetically)
Outer Envelope: Mr. Michael Knight
                          Ms. Paula Orlandi

Two Sisters (over 16)
Inner Envelope: The Misses Smith
Outer Envelope: The Misses Mary and Jane Smith
                          (in order of age)

Two Brothers (over 16)
Inner Envelope: The Messrs. Smith
Outer Envelope: The Messrs. John and Glen Smith
                          (in order of age)

Brothers & Sisters (over 16)
Inner Envelope: Mary, Jane, John & Glen
                          (name the girls first, in order of age)
Outer Envelope: The Misses Smith
                          The Messrs. Smith
                          (name the girls first)

A Brother and Sister (over 16)
Inner Envelope: Jane and John
                          (name the girl first)
Outer Envelope: Miss Jane Smith and
                          Mr. John Smith
                          (name the girl first)

GUIDELINES FOR ADDRESSING INVITATIONS

Note: Inner envelope does not include first names or addresses.
The outer envelope includes first names and addresses.

Widow
Inner Envelope: Mrs. Smith
Outer Envelope: Mrs. William Smith

Divorcee
Inner Envelope: Mrs. Smith
Outer Envelope: Mrs. Jones Smith
                    (maiden name and former husband's surname)

Reception

THE RECEPTION IS A PARTY WHERE ALL YOUR guests come together to celebrate your new life as a married couple. It should reflect and complement the formality of your ceremony. The selection of a reception site will depend on its availability, price, proximity to the ceremony site, and the number of people it will accommodate.

RECEPTION SITE FEE

There are two basic types of reception sites. The first type charges a per person fee that includes the facility, food, tables, silverware, china, and so forth. Examples: hotels, restaurants, and catered yachts. The second type charges a room rental fee and you are responsible for providing the food, beverages, linens, and possibly tables and chairs. Examples: clubs, halls, parks, museums, and private homes.

The advantage of the first type is that almost everything is done for you. The disadvantage, however, is that your choices of food, china, and linen are limited. Usually you are not permitted to bring in an outside caterer and must select from a predetermined menu.

Options: Private homes, gardens, hotels, clubs, restaurants, halls, parks, museums, yachts, and wineries are some of the more popular choices for receptions.

Things to Consider: When comparing the cost of different locations, consider the rental fee, food, beverages, parking, gratuity, setup charges, and the cost of rental equipment needed such as tables, chairs, canopies, and so forth.

If you are planning an outdoor reception, be sure to have a backup site in case of rain.

Beware: Some hotels are known for double booking. A bride may reserve the largest or most elegant room in a hotel for her reception, only to find out later that the hotel took the liberty to book a more profitable event in the room she had reserved and moved her reception over to a smaller or less elegant room.

Also be careful of hotels that book events too close together. You don't want your guests to wait outside while your room is being set up for the reception. And you don't want to be "forced out" before you are ready to leave because the hotel needs to arrange the room for the next reception. Get your rental hours and the name of your room in writing.

Tips to Save Money: Since the cost of the reception is approximately 35% of the total cost of your wedding, you can save the most money by limiting your guest list. If you hire a wedding consultant, he or she may be able to cut your cake and save you the cake-cutting fee. Check this out with your facility or caterer. Reception sites that charge a room rental fee may waive this fee if you meet minimum requirements on food and beverages consumed. Try to negotiate this before you book the facility.

Price Range: $300 - $5,000

HORS D'OEUVRES

At receptions where a full meal is to be served, hors d'oeuvres may be offered to guests during the first hour of the reception. However, at a tea or cocktail reception, hors d'oeuvres will be the "main course."

Options: There are many options for hors d'oeuvres, depending on the formality of your reception and the type of food to be served at the meal. Popular items are foods that can easily be picked up and eaten with one hand. Hors d'oeuvres may be set out on tables "buffet style" for guests to help themselves, or they may be passed around on trays by waiters and waitresses.

Things to Consider: When selecting hors d'oeuvres for your reception, consider whether heating or refrigeration will be available and choose your food accordingly. When planning your menu, consider the time of day. You should select lighter hors d'oeuvres for a midday reception and heavier hors d'oeuvres for an evening reception.

Tips to Save Money: Tray pass hors d'oeuvres during cocktail hour and serve a lighter meal. Avoid serving hors d'oeuvres that are labor intensive or that require expensive ingredients. Compare two or three caterers; there is a wide price range between caterers for the same food. Compare the total cost of catering (main entree plus hors d'oeuvres) when selecting a caterer. Consider serving hors d'oeuvres buffet style. Your guests will eat less this way than if waiters and waitresses are constantly serving them hors d'oeuvres.

Price Range: $3 - $20 per person

MAIN MEAL/CATERER

If your reception is going to be at a hotel, restaurant or other facility that provides food, you will need to select a meal to serve your guests. Most of these facilities will have a predetermined menu from which to select your meal. If your reception is going to be in a facility that does not provide food, you will need to hire an outside caterer. The caterer will be responsible for preparing, cooking, and serving the food. The caterer will also be responsible for beverages and for cleaning up after the event. Before signing a contract, make sure you understand all the services the caterer will provide. Your contract should state the amount and type of food and beverages that will be served, the way in which they will be served, the number of servers who will be available, and the cost per food item or person.

Options: Food can be served either buffet style or as a sit-down meal. It should be chosen according to the time of day, year, and formality of the wedding. Although there are many main dishes to choose from, chicken and beef are the most popular selections for a large event. Ask your facility manager or caterer for their specialty. If you have a special type of food you would like to serve at your reception, select a facility or caterer who specializes in preparing it.

Things to Consider: When hiring a caterer, check to see if the location for

GREEN WEDDING TIP

Seasonal Menu Suggestions— Spring Though it is only the third most popular season in which to get married, caterers still have a lot of fun with spring wedding dishes because of the fresh, young vegetables available at this time. Baby carrots, haricot verts, baby asparagus, new potatoes, and sugar snap peas are all springtime offerings that add color to a plate and flair to an appetizer. Rhubarb, pomegranates, mango, and apricots are also abundant this time of year and can be featured in salads, glazes, sauces, pies, cookies, or petit fours.

GREEN WEDDING TIP

Seasonal Menu Suggestions— Summer If you are getting married in summertime, you're not alone— according to the Association of Bridal Consultants, the summer months account for around 40 percent of all weddings. Feature fresh fruit and vegetables in all your summer wedding dishes. Salads should include sliced berries, and if you serve a soup course, make sure it is chilled. Main dishes should be light and also incorporate fruit, such as grilled pears or pineapple. Be sure to add fresh lemonade to your drink menu, too.

your reception provides refrigeration and cooking equipment. If not, make sure your caterer is fully self-supported with portable refrigeration and heating equipment. A competent caterer will prepare much of the food in his or her own kitchen and should provide an adequate staff of cooks, servers, and bartenders. Ask for references and look at photos from previous parties so you know how the food will be presented; or better yet, visit an event they are catering.

Beware: Avoid mayonnaise, cream sauces, or custard fillings if food must go unrefrigerated for any length of time.

Tips to Save Money: Give only 85 to 95 percent of your final guest count to your caterer or facility manager, depending on how certain you are that all of your guests who have responded will come. Chances are that several, if not many, of your guests will not show up. But if they do, your caterer should have enough food for all of them. This is especially true with buffet-style receptions, in which case the facility or caterer will charge extra for each additional guest. However, if you give a complete count of your guests to your caterer and some of them don't show up, you will still have to pay for their plates. If offering a buffet meal, have the catering staff serve the food onto guests' plates rather than allowing guests to serve themselves. This will help to regulate the amount of food consumed.

Select food that is not too time-consuming to prepare, or food that does not have expensive ingredients. Also, consider a brunch or early afternoon wedding so the reception will fall between meals, allowing

GREEN WEDDING TIP

Seasonal Menu Suggestions—Autumn Because of the crisp weather, gorgeous colors, and abundance of produce, fall is the second most popular season in which to hold a wedding. Like summer, you will have a bounty of items to choose from. For appetizers, consider baked brie and cranberry purses or skewered butternut squash bites done in a brown sugar glaze. A soothing pumpkin bisque served in hollowed-out bowls made from halved acorn squashes is a wonderful touch for a soup course. Hot apple cider and apple pies should be featured on your dessert table.

GREEN WEDDING TIP

Ocean-Friendly Serve fish and seafood that are not overfished, endangered, or high in mercury. According to the Seafood Watch List, the following fishes are to be avoided: Chilean Seabass, Atlantic Cod, King Crab, mahi mahi, Orange Roughy, farmed Atlantic Salmon, any type of shark or imported shrimp, Bigeye or Yellowfin Tuna, and Yellowtail. Better environmental bets are abalone, Alaska wild salmon, bay scallops, Dungeness Crab, Skipjack tuna, white seabass, rainbow trout, and farmed varieties of catfish, clams, mussels, and oysters.

you to serve hors d'oeuvres instead of a full meal. Or tray pass hors d'oeuvres during cocktail hour and choose a lighter meal.

Price Range: $20 - $100 per person

LIQUOR/BEVERAGES

Prices for liquor and beverages vary greatly, depending on the amount and brand of alcohol served. Traditionally, at least champagne or punch should be served to toast the couple.

Options: White and red wines, scotch, vodka, gin, rum, and beer are the most popular alcoholic beverages. Sodas and fruit punch are popular nonalcoholic beverages served at receptions. And of course, don't forget coffee or tea. There are a number of options and variations for serving alcoholic beverages: a full open bar where you pay for your guests to drink as much as they wish; an open bar for the first hour, followed by a cash bar where guests pay for their own drinks; cash bar only; beer and wine only; nonalcoholic beverages only; or any combination thereof.

Things to Consider: If you plan to serve alcoholic beverages at a reception site that does not provide liquor, make sure your caterer has a license to serve alcohol and that your reception site allows alcoholic beverages. If you plan to order your own alcohol, do so three or four weeks before the event. If you plan to have a no-host or "cash" bar, consider notifying your guests so they know to bring cash with them. A simple line that says "No-Host Bar" on the reception card should suffice.

GREEN WEDDING TIP

Biodegradable Dishes

Serving more than 100 people appetizers, dinner, and dessert racks up a lot of dishes that need to be washed and dried, which wastes energy and water. And yet you may have written off disposable dishes, thinking they will sit in a landfill long after death parts you and your loved one. Not so! Choose biodegradable plates and utensils made from potato, corn, or sugar cane. Most varieties are elegant looking and sturdy enough to keep your wedding from feeling like a picnic.

In selecting the type of alcohol to serve, consider the age and preference of your guests, the type of food that will be served, and the time of day your guests will be drinking.

On the average, you should allow one drink per person, per hour at the reception. A bottle of champagne will usually serve six glasses. Never serve liquor without some type of food.

Use the following chart to plan your beverage needs:

Beverages	Amount based on 100 guests
Bourbon	3 Fifths
Gin	3 Fifths
Rum	2 Fifths
Scotch	4 Quarts
Vodka	5 Quarts
White Wine	2 Cases
Red Wine	1 Case
Champagne	3 Cases
Other	2 Cases each: Club Soda, Seltzer Water, Tonic Water, Ginger Ale, Cola, Beer

GREEN WEDDING TIP

Leave Only Love Behind

Go the extra mile and aim to do without as many dishes as possible. Serve sushi or small appetizers in long cucumber cups, salad in hollowed-out melon bowls, and dips and salsas in pineapple halves. Soup, too, can be served in hollowed-out squash bowls and plates can be fashioned out of sturdy, well-cleaned banana leaves. These options are most realistic for small weddings of under 30 people—but that size guest list is optimal for a truly eco-friendly wedding anyway.

If you are hosting an open bar at a hotel or restaurant, ask the catering manager how they charge for liquor: by consumption or by number of bottles opened. Get this in writing before the event and then ask for a full consumption report after the event.

Beware: In today's society, it is not uncommon for the hosts of a party to be held legally responsible for the conduct and safety of their guests. Keep this in mind when planning the quantity and type of beverages to serve. Also, be sure to remind your bartenders not to serve alcohol to minors.

Tips to Save Money: To keep beverage costs down, serve punch, wine, or nonalcoholic drinks only. If your caterer allows it, consider buying liquor from a wholesaler who will let you return unopened bottles.

GREEN WEDDING TIP

Eco-Friendly Table Settings
Make sure your tables are as earth-friendly as the food served on them. Set tables with organic cotton linens and napkins or ones made from recycled or biodegradable materials. Rather than ordering plastic knick-knacks made in China, use natural items to hold guest place cards, such as river rocks, seashells, pine cones or small pumpkins. Or, just print them out on small pieces of recycled stationery and attach them to a clothesline using wooden clothespins—this simple and eco-friendly set-up has a quaint, rustic look to it.

GREEN WEDDING TIP

Drink as the Locals Do
Consuming locally is the new tenet of the environmental movement. When you consume products that are produced locally, you support small business and reduce the pollution and expense associated with long-distance shipping. With this in mind, serve a locally produced organic wine or beer at your wedding. Small-scale wineries have sprung up in surprising areas around the country, from Maine to Kentucky to Minnesota (see www.allamericanwineries.com for a complete list). Likewise, craft breweries are all the rage and many produce interesting and delicious beers at a great price.

Host alcoholic beverages for the first hour, then go to a cash bar. Or host beer, wine, and soft drinks only and have mixed drinks available on a cash basis. The bartending fee is often waived if you meet the minimum requirements on beverages consumed. For the toast, tray pass champagne only to those guests who want it, not to everyone. Many people will make a toast with whatever they are currently drinking. Consider serving sparkling cider in place of champagne.

Omit waiters and waitresses. Instead, have an open bar in which your guests have to get their own drinks. People tend to drink almost twice as much if there are waiters and waitresses constantly asking them if they would like another drink and then bringing drinks to them.

Price Range: $8 - $35 per person

BARTENDING/BAR SETUP FEE

Some reception sites and caterers charge an extra fee for bartending and for setting up the bar.

Tips to Save Money: The bartending fee could be and often is waived if you meet a minimum requirement on beverages consumed. Try to negotiate this with your caterer prior to hiring him/her.

Price Range: $75 - $500

GREEN WEDDING TIP

Celebrate with Cork
When making beverage selections, choose wine bottles that have real corks. According to a report in the British newspaper *The Independent*, the increasing use of screw-top bottles has driven down the demand for cork—and subsequently, its price. As a result, farmers in some areas of the world are using unsustainable farming methods to harvest cork because it saves them money to do so. In turn, these forests are being destroyed, and the animals that make their homes there are becoming endangered.

GREEN WEDDING TIP

Avoid the Bottle and Can
When interviewing catering companies and bartenders, ask if they can serve tap water and fountain drinks rather than bottled waters or sodas. Likewise, look into getting a keg of beer that can be served on tap, rather than offering individual bottles. Your goal is to reduce the number of bottles and cans that need to be used. If bottles and cans are unavoidable, set up recycling bins near the bar and make sure the venue you select allows them to be recycled.

CORKAGE FEE

Many reception sites and caterers make money by marking up the food and alcohol they sell. You may wish to provide your own alcohol for several reasons. First, it is more cost effective. Second, you may want to serve an exotic wine or champagne that the reception site or caterer does not offer. In either case, and if your reception site or caterer allows it, be prepared to pay a corkage fee. This is the fee for each bottle brought into the reception site and opened by a member of their staff.

Things to Consider: You need to consider

Price Range: $0.25 - $1 per person

SERVICE PROVIDERS' MEALS

Things to Consider: It is considered a courtesy to feed your photographer, videographer, and any other "service provider" at the reception. Check options and prices with your caterer or reception site manager. Make sure you allocate a place for your service providers to eat. You may want them to eat with your guests, or you may prefer setting a place outside the main room for them to eat. Your service providers may be more comfortable with the latter.

Tips to Save Money: You don't need to

whether the expenses saved after paying the corkage fee justify the hassle and liability of bringing in your own alcohol.

Price Range: $5 - $20 per bottle

FEE TO POUR COFFEE

In addition to corkage and cake-cutting fees, some facilities also charge extra to pour coffee with the wedding cake.

Things to Consider: Again, when comparing the cost of various reception sites, don't forget to add up all the extra miscellaneous costs, such as the fee for pouring coffee.

feed your service providers the same meal as your guests. You can order sandwiches or another less expensive meal for them. If the meal is a buffet, there should be enough food left after all your guests have been served for your service providers to eat. Tell them they are welcome to eat after all your guests have been served. Be sure to discuss this with your catering manager.

Price Range: $10 - $30 per person

GRATUITY

It is customary to pay a gratuity fee to your caterer. The average gratuity is 15 percent to 20 percent of your food and beverage bill.

Tips to Save Money: Ask about these costs up front and select your caterer or reception site accordingly.

Price Range: 15 - 25 percent of total food and beverage bill

PARTY FAVORS

Party favors are gift items given to your guests as mementos of your wedding. They add a very special touch to your wedding and can become keepsakes for your guests.

Options: White matchboxes engraved with the couple's names and wedding date; cocktail napkins marked in the same way;

GREEN WEDDING TIP

Give Your Guests the Gift of Charity
Eco-friendly brides and grooms are increasingly forgoing party favors and opting to make a donation to charity instead. Pick any charity you and your partner care about— for the comfort of your guests, choose an environmental, social, or medical one rather than a political one. On recycled or plantable paper, print up cards that let your guests know you are donating in their honor in lieu of a traditional favor. These can double as table setting cards, too. Spread your money around by assigning each table a different charity.

GREEN WEDDING TIP

Carbon Offset Your Wedding
The average wedding emits approximately 14.5 tons of CO_2 into the atmosphere. When you consider that the average person emits 12 tons of CO_2 over the course of a whole year, it becomes clear that weddings leave a heavy carbon footprint. Counteract the carbon impact of your wedding by giving your guests carbon offset credits instead of favors. These can be purchased from organizations such as Climate Care or TerraPass.com, who use the money to fund eco-friendly projects that fight climate change.

individually wrapped and marked chocolates, almonds, or fine candy are all popular party favors. Wine or champagne bottles marked with the bride and groom's names and wedding date on a personalized label are also very popular. These come in different sizes and can be purchased by the case.

Things to Consider: Personalized favors need to be ordered several weeks in advance.

Price Range: $1 - $25 per person

ONLINE PHOTO ALBUM

Save money by skipping the disposable cameras. These days, most guests will bring their own digital cameras — which take much sharper, clearer photos than their cardboard counterparts, anyhow. Create an online photo album where guests can go to upload their digital photos for all to see.

Options: There are many free websites that allow you to create an online, shareable photo gallery, including Flickr, Snapfish, Picasa and Photobucket. Create a URL, login and password for your wedding gallery. Then, hand out small cards with this information at your wedding, or email the information to all your guests after the wedding so everyone can upload the photos they took.

Price Range: Free

ROSE PETALS/RICE

Rose petals or rice are traditionally tossed over the bride and groom as they leave the church after the ceremony or when they leave the reception. This tradition was initiated in the Middle Ages whereby a handful of wheat was thrown over the bridal couple as a symbol of fertility. Rose petals are used to symbolize happiness, beauty, and prosperity.

Options: Rose petals, rice, or confetti is often used. However, an environmentally correct alternative is to use grass or flower seeds, which do not need to be cleaned up if tossed over a grassy area.

Things to Consider: Rose petals can stain carpets; rice can sting faces, harm birds and make stairs dangerously slippery; confetti is messy and hard to clean. Clubs and hotels seldom permit the use of any of these. Ask about their policy.

Price Range: $0.35 - $2 per person

GIFT ATTENDANT

The gift attendant is responsible for watching over your gifts during the reception so that no one walks away with them. This is necessary only if your reception is held in a public area such as a hotel or outside garden where strangers may be walking by. It is not proper to have a friend or family member take on this duty as he or she would not enjoy the reception. The gift attendant should also be responsible for transporting your gifts from the reception site to your car or bridal suite.

Tips to Save Money: Hire a young boy or girl from your neighborhood to watch over your gifts at the reception.

Price Range: $20 - $100

PARKING FEE/VALET SERVICES

Many reception sites charge for parking. It is customary, although not necessary, for the host of the wedding to pay this charge. At a large home reception, you should consider hiring a professional, qualified valet service if parking could be a problem. If so, make sure the valet service is fully insured.

Tips to Save Money: To save money, let your guests pay their own parking fees.

Price Range: $3 - $10 per car

GREEN WEDDING TIP

Watch What You Toss

There are several eco-friendly alternatives to tossing rice, flower petals, or confetti during your ceremony. Instead of confetti—which is made with bleaches and dyes—or rice—which swells in the stomachs of birds that eat it—you can use grass seed, flower seeds, or shaved coconut. These natural items often come wrapped in attractive, recyclable baggies. If you have your heart set on confetti, check out an eco-friendly kind called Ecofetti. It's made from biodegradable materials that dissolve easily and quickly in water.

RECEPTION SITE COMPARISON CHART

Questions	POSSIBILITY 1
What is the name of the reception site?	
What is the website and e-mail of the reception site?	
What is the address of the reception site?	
What is the name and phone number of my contact person?	
What dates and times are available?	
What is the maximum number of guests for a seated reception?	
What is the maximum number of guests for a cocktail reception?	
What is the reception site fee?	
What is the price range for a seated lunch?	
What is the price range for a buffet lunch?	
What is the price range for a seated dinner?	
What is the price range for a buffet dinner?	
What is the corkage fee?	
What is the cake-cutting fee?	
What is the ratio of servers to guests?	
How much time will be allotted for my reception?	
What music restrictions are there, if any?	

POSSIBILITY 2	POSSIBILITY 3

RECEPTION SITE COMPARISON CHART

Questions	POSSIBILITY 1
What alcohol restrictions are there, if any?	
Are there any restrictions for rice or rose petal tossing?	
What room and table decorations are available?	
Is a changing room available?	
Is there handicap accessibility?	
Is a dance floor included in the site fee?	
Are tables, chairs, and linens included in the site fee?	
Are outside caterers allowed?	
Are kitchen facilities available for outside caterers?	
Does the facility have full liability insurance?	
What perks or giveaways are offered?	
How many parking spaces are available for my wedding party?	
How many parking spaces are available for my guests?	
What is the cost for parking, if any?	
What is the cost for sleeping rooms, if available?	
What is the payment policy?	
What is the cancellation policy?	

POSSIBILITY 2	POSSIBILITY 3

RECEPTION SITE INFORMATION SHEET

RECEPTION SITE:

Site Coordinator: _____ Cost: _____

Website: _____

E-mail: _____

Phone: _____ Fax: _____

Address: _____

City: _____ State: _____ Zip: _____

Name of Room: _____ Room Capacity: _____

Date Confirmed: _____ Confirm Head Count By: _____

Beginning Time: _____ Ending Time: _____

Cocktails/Hors d'Oeuvres Time: _____ Meal Time: _____

Color of Linens: _____ Color of Napkins: _____

Total Cost: _____

Deposit: _____ Date: _____

Balance: _____ Date Due: _____

Cancellation Policy: _____

EQUIPMENT INCLUDES:

❑ Tables   ❑ Chairs   ❑ Linens   ❑ Tableware
❑ Barware   ❑ Heaters   ❑ Electric Outlet   ❑ Musical Instruments

SERVICE INCLUDES:

❑ Waiters   ❑ Bartenders   ❑ Valet   ❑ Main Meal
❑ Clean Up   ❑ Setup   ❑ Security   ❑ Free Parking

CATERER:

Contact Person: _____   Cost Per Person: _____

Website: _____

E-mail: _____

Phone: _____   Fax: _____

Address: _____

City: _____ State: _____   Zip: _____

Confirmed Date: _____   Confirm Head Count By: _____

Arrival Time: _____   Departure Time: _____

Cocktails/Hors d'Oeuvres Time: _____   Meal Time: _____

Color of Linens: _____   Color of Napkins: _____

Total Cost: _____

Deposit: _____ Date: _____

Balance: _____   Date Due: _____

Cancellation Policy: _____

EQUIPMENT INCLUDES:

❏ Tables   ❏ Chairs   ❏ Linens   ❏ Tableware
❏ Barware   ❏ Heaters   ❏ Lighting   ❏ Candles

SERVICE INCLUDES:

❏ Waiters   ❏ Bartenders   ❏ Setup   ❏ Clean Up
❏ Security   ❏ Hors d'Oeuvres   ❏ Buffet Meal   ❏ Seated Meal
❏ Cocktails   ❏ Champagne   ❏ Wine   ❏ Beer
❏ Punch   ❏ Soft Drinks   ❏ Coffee/Tea   ❏ Cake

TABLE SEATING ARRANGEMENTS

Complete this form only after finalizing your guest list.

Head Table	Bride's Family Table	Groom's Family Table
_____	_____	_____
_____	_____	_____
_____	_____	_____
_____	_____	_____
_____	_____	_____
_____	_____	_____
_____	_____	_____
_____	_____	_____
_____	_____	_____

• Table _____	• Table _____	• Table _____
_____	_____	_____
_____	_____	_____
_____	_____	_____
_____	_____	_____
_____	_____	_____
_____	_____	_____
_____	_____	_____
_____	_____	_____

• Table _____	• Table _____	• Table _____
_____	_____	_____
_____	_____	_____
_____	_____	_____
_____	_____	_____
_____	_____	_____
_____	_____	_____
_____	_____	_____
_____	_____	_____

TABLE SEATING ARRANGEMENTS

Complete this form only after finalizing your guest list.

• Table _____

_____
_____
_____
_____
_____
_____
_____
_____

• Table _____

_____
_____
_____
_____
_____
_____
_____
_____

• Table _____

_____
_____
_____
_____
_____
_____
_____
_____

• Table _____

_____
_____
_____
_____
_____
_____
_____
_____

• Table _____

_____
_____
_____
_____
_____
_____
_____
_____

• Table _____

_____
_____
_____
_____
_____
_____
_____
_____

• Table _____

_____
_____
_____
_____
_____
_____
_____
_____

• Table _____

_____
_____
_____
_____
_____
_____
_____
_____

• Table _____

_____
_____
_____
_____
_____
_____
_____
_____

LIQUOR ORDER FORM

Liquor Store: _____   Date Ordered: _____

Salesperson: _____   Phone: _____

Website: _____

E-mail: _____

Address: _____

City: _____   State: _____   Zip: _____

Cost: _____

Delivered By: _____   Delivery Date: _____

Type of Liquor:	# of Bottles:	Price:

Type of Favor	Website/Company	Quantity	Price
White matchboxes engraved with names of bride and groom and date of the wedding			
Cocktail napkins engraved with names of the bride and groom and date of the wedding			
Almonds, chocolates, or other fine candy			
Customized wine or champagne labels with bride and groom's names and wedding date			
Porcelain or ceramic favors with bride and groom's names and wedding date			
Plant or tree shoot to be planted in honor of the bride and groom			
Other:			
Other:			
Other:			
Other:			

CATERER COMPARISON CHART

Questions	POSSIBILITY 1
What is the name of the caterer?	
What is the website and e-mail of the caterer?	
What is the address of the caterer?	
What is the name and phone number of my contact person?	
How many years have you been in business?	
What percentage of your business is dedicated to receptions?	
Do you have liability insurance/license to serve alcohol?	
When is the final head-count needed?	
What is your ratio of servers to guests?	
How do your servers dress for wedding receptions?	
Price range for a seated lunch/buffet lunch?	
Price range for a seated/buffet dinner?	
How much gratuity is expected?	
What is your cake-cutting fee?	
What is your bartending fee?	
What is your fee to clean up after the reception?	
What is your payment/cancellation policy?	

POSSIBILITY 2	POSSIBILITY 3

MENU WORKSHEET

HORS D'OEUVRES: _____

_____

_____

_____

SALADS/APPETIZERS: _____

_____

_____

_____

SOUPS: _____

_____

_____

_____

MAIN ENTREE: _____

_____

_____

_____

DESSERTS: _____

_____

_____

_____

WEDDING CAKE: _____

_____

_____

_____

Music

MUSIC IS A MAJOR PART OF YOUR wedding ceremony and reception. Music helps set the tone and mood of each portion of the day, whether you want guests quietly watching the processional, mingling and enjoying cocktails, or having a blast on the dance floor.

CEREMONY MUSIC

Ceremony music is the music played during the prelude, processional, ceremony, recessional, and postlude. Prelude music is played while guests are being seated, 15 to 30 minutes before the ceremony begins. Processional music is played as the wedding party enters the ceremony site. Recessional music is played as the wedding party leaves the ceremony site. Postlude music is played while the guests leave the ceremony site.

Options: The most traditional musical instrument for wedding ceremonies is the organ. But guitars, pianos, flutes, harps, and violins are also popular today.

Popular selections for a Christian wedding:
Trumpet Voluntary by Purcell
The Bridal Chorus by Wagner
Wedding March by Mendelssohn
Postlude in G Major by Handel
Canon in D Major by Pachelbel
Adagio in A Minor by Bach

Popular selections for a Jewish wedding:
Erev Shel Shoshanim
Erev Ba
Hana' Ava Babanot

Things to Consider: Music may or may not be included as part of the ceremony site fee. Be sure to check with your ceremony site about restrictions pertaining to music and the availability of musical instruments for your use. Discuss the selection of ceremony music with your officiant and musicians. Make sure the musicians know how to play the selections you request.

When selecting ceremony music, keep in mind the formality of your wedding, your religious affiliation, and the length of the ceremony. Also consider the location and time of day. If the ceremony is outside where there may be other noises such as traffic, wind, or people's voices, or if a large number of guests will be attending your ceremony, consider having the music, your officiant, and your vows amplified. Make sure there are electrical outlets close to where the instruments will be set up.

Tips to Save Money: Hire student musicians from your local university or high school. Ask a friend to sing or play at your ceremony; they will be honored. If you're planning to hire a band for your reception, consider hiring a scaled-down version of the same band to play at your ceremony, such as a trio of flute, guitar, and vocals. This could enable you to negotiate a "package" price. If you're planning to hire a DJ for your reception, consider hiring him/her to play pre-recorded music at your ceremony.

Price Range: $100 - $900

RECEPTION MUSIC

Special songs will make your reception unique. When you select music for your reception, keep in mind the age and musical preference of your guests, your budget, and any restrictions that the reception site may have. Bands and musicians are typically more expensive than DJ's.

Options: There are many options for reception music: you can hire a DJ, a band, an orchestra, or any combination of one or more instruments and vocalists.

Things to Consider: Hire an entertainment agency that can help you choose a reliable DJ or band that will play the type of music you want. Whoever you choose, they should have experience performing at wedding receptions.

If you want your musician to act as a master of ceremonies, make sure he or she has a complete timeline for your reception in order to announce the various events such as the toasts, first dance, and cutting of the cake. Consider watching your musicians perform at another event before booking their services.

If you need a large variety of music to satisfy all your guests, consider hiring a DJ. A professional DJ can play any type of music and may even offer a light show. Make sure you give him/her a list of the songs you want played at your reception and the sequence in which you want them played. Make sure there are electrical outlets at the reception site close to where the musicians will be performing.

Tips to Save Money: You will probably get a better price if you hire a band or DJ directly than if you hire them through an entertainment agency. Check the music department of local colleges and universities for names of student musicians and DJs. You may be able to hire a student for a fraction of the price of a professional musician or DJ. A DJ is typically less expensive than a "live" musician. Some facilities have contracts with certain DJ's, and you may be able to save money by hiring one of them.

Price Range: $500 - $5,000

Bonus Tip: For suggestions on appropriate music for each moment of the wedding, you should consider purchasing *The Ultimate Guide to Wedding Music* from Wedding Solutions. This books contain lyrics for 100 of the most popular love songs for weddings. It also includes an audio CD with excerpts from 99 of the most popular classical music pieces for weddings.

CEREMONY MUSIC COMPARISON CHART

Questions	POSSIBILITY 1
What is the name of the musician or band?	
What is the website and e-mail of the musician or band?	
What is the address of the musician or band?	
What is the name and phone number of my contact person?	
How many years of professional experience do you have?	
What percentage of your business is dedicated to weddings?	
Are you the person who will perform at my wedding?	
What instrument(s) do you play/What type of music do you specialize in?	
What are your hourly fees?	
What is the cost of a soloist?	
What is the cost of a duet?	
What is the cost of a trio?	
What is the cost of a quartet?	
How would you dress for my wedding?	
Do you have liability insurance?	
Do you have a cordless microphone?	
What is your payment/cancellation policy?	

CEREMONY MUSIC COMPARISON CHART

POSSIBILITY 2	POSSIBILITY 3

RECEPTION MUSIC COMPARISON CHART

Questions	POSSIBILITY 1
What is the name of the musician? Band? DJ?	
What is the website and e-mail of the company?	
What is the address of the company?	
What is the name and phone number of my contact person?	
How many years of professional experience do you have?	
What percentage of your business is dedicated to receptions?	
How many people are in your band?	
What type of music do you specialize in?	
What type of sound system do you have?	
Can you act as a master of ceremonies? How do you dress?	
Can you provide a light show?	
Do you have a cordless microphone?	
How many breaks do you take? How long are they?	
Do you play recorded music during breaks?	
Do you have liability insurance?	
What are your fees for a 4-hour reception?	
What is your cost for each additional hour?	

POSSIBILITY 2	POSSIBILITY 3

CEREMONY MUSIC SELECTIONS

Make a copy of this form and give it to your musicians.

When	Selection	Composer	Played By
Prelude 1			
Prelude 2			
Prelude 3			
Processional			
Bride's Processional			
Ceremony 1			
Ceremony 2			
Ceremony 3			
Recessional			
Postlude			
Other:			
Other:			
Other:			
Other:			
Other:			
Other:			
Other:			

Make a copy of this form and give it to your musicians.

When	Selection	Songwriter	Played By
Receiving Line			
During Hors d'Oeuvres			
During Dinner			
First Dance			
Second Dance			
Third Dance			
Bouquet Toss			
Garter Removal			
Cutting of the Cake			
Last Dance			
Couple Leaving			
Other:			
Other:			
Other:			
Other:			
Other:			
Other:			

WEDDING PLANNING NOTES

Bakery

WEDDING CAKES MAY BE ORDERED FROM a caterer or from a bakery. Some hotels and restaurants may also be able to provide a wedding cake. However, you will probably be better off ordering your cake from a bakery that specializes in wedding cakes. Ask to see photographs of other wedding cakes your baker has created, and by all means, ask for a tasting!

WEDDING CAKE

Options: When ordering your cake, you will have to decide not only on a flavor, but also on a size, shape, and color. Size is determined by the number of guests. You can choose from one large tier or more smaller tiers. The cake can be round, square, or heart-shaped. The most common flavors are chocolate, carrot, lemon, rum, and "white" cakes. You can be creative by adding a filling to your cake, such as custard, strawberry, or chocolate. You may also want to consider having tiers of different flavors.

Things to Consider: Price, workmanship, quality, and taste vary considerably from baker to baker. In addition to flavor, size, and cost, consider decoration and spoilage (sugar keeps longer than cream frostings). The cake should be beautifully displayed on its own table decorated with flowers or greenery. Make sure the baker, caterer, or reception site manager can provide you with a pretty cake-cutting knife. If not, you will need to purchase or rent one.

When determining the size of the cake, don't forget that you'll be saving the top tier for your first anniversary. This top tier should be removed before the cake is cut, wrapped in several layers of plastic wrap or put inside a plastic container, and kept frozen until your anniversary.

Tips to Save Money: Some bakers have setup and delivery fees, and some don't. Check for individuals who bake from their home. They are usually more reasonable, but you should check with your local health department before hiring one of these at-home bakers. Also, some caterers have contracts with bakeries and can pass on savings to you. Some bakeries require a deposit on columns and plates; other bakeries use disposable columns and plates, saving you the rental fee and the hassle of returning these items.

Price Range: $2 - $12 per piece

GREEN WEDDING TIP

Skip Dessert Plates
Minimize the number of dishes used during your wedding by making the dessert course a finger-food-only event. Offer bite-sized, plate-less desserts such as cupcakes, cookies, brownies or petit fours. Your guests will only need to use recycled or cloth napkins to wipe the delicious crumbs from their lips! Further reduce the amount of waste by creating a dessert bar where guests can go up and get what they want, rather than being served a pre-set assortment that might go uneaten.

GREEN WEDDING TIP

Enlist a Friend to Act as Baker
Rather than hiring a professional to bake your wedding cake, ask a friend to bake one for you. Baking a cake or cupcakes in a home stove consumes much less energy than a professional commercial oven does. Plus, you have control over which ingredients are used, and can select free-range eggs and organic milk, sugar, and flour. By transporting the cake to the reception in a private car, you cut down on the energy consumed by a chilled delivery truck. Whichever friend you ask will be honored to give you this special and delicious gift.

GROOM'S CAKE

The groom's cake is an old Southern tradition whereby this cake is cut up and distributed to guests in little white boxes engraved with the bride and groom's names. Today the groom's cake, if offered, is cut and served along with the wedding cake.

Options: Usually a chocolate cake decorated with fruit.

Tips to Save Money: Because of its cost and the labor involved in cutting and distributing the cake, very few people offer this delightful custom anymore.

Price Range: $1 - $2 per piece

CAKE DELIVERY/SETUP FEE

This is the fee charged by bakers to deliver and set up your wedding cake at the reception site. It usually includes a deposit on the cake pillars and plate which will be refunded upon their return to the baker.

Tips to Save Money: Have a friend or family member get a quick lesson on how to set up your cake. Have them pick it up and set it up the day of your wedding, then have the florist decorate the cake and/or cake table with flowers and greenery.

Price Range: $40 - $100

GREEN WEDDING TIP

Eco-Friendly Cake Toppers
Don't bother with a generic toss-away cake topper made from plastic. Top your cake with something biodegradable but decorative, such as edible flower petals, leaves, or candies. Also, forgo any cake decorations made from inorganic materials, such as fake pearls. Most quality bakers can use real sugar to craft cake decorations in the shape of seashells, flowers, designs, animals or leaves that will stun your guests and are also completely digestible and delicious.

GREEN WEDDING TIP

Put Yourself on Your Cake
Only buy a cake topper if it is something you will love to look at forever. A fantastic example comes from We Bobble (www.webobble.com), a company that makes sculpted cake topper bobblehead dolls that look exactly like you and your partner. You send them a photograph, and they create three-dimensional dolls that you and your partner will love to keep on display in your home long after your cake has been eaten. Or, visit the ever-popular handmade craft site Etsy.com and search for personalizable cake toppers.

CAKE-CUTTING FEE

Most reception sites and caterers charge a fee for each slice of cake they cut if the cake is brought in from an outside bakery. This fee will probably shock you. It is simply their way of enticing you to order the cake through them. Unfortunately, many caterers will not allow a member of your party to cut the cake.

Tips to Save Money: Many hotels and restaurants include a dessert in the cost of their meal packages. If you forego this dessert and substitute your cake as the dessert, they may be willing to waive the cake-cutting fee. Be sure to ask them.

Price Range: $0.75 - $2.50 per person

CAKE TOP

The bride's cake is often topped and surrounded with fresh flowers, but traditional "cake tops" (figurines set atop the wedding cake) are also very popular.

Options: Bells, love birds, a bridal couple or replica of two wedding rings are popular choices for cake tops and can be saved as mementos of your wedding day.

Beware: Some porcelain and other heavier cake tops need to be anchored down into the cake. If you're planning to use a cake top other than flowers, be sure to discuss this with your baker.

Tips to Save Money: Borrow a cake top from a friend or a family member as "something borrowed," an age-old wedding tradition.

Price Range: $20 - $150

CAKE KNIFE/TOASTING GLASSES

Your cake knife and toasting glasses should complement your overall setting; these items will bring you happy memories of your wedding day every time you use them. The cake knife is used to cut the cake at the reception. The bride usually cuts the first two slices of the wedding cake with the groom's hand placed over hers. The groom feeds the bride first. Then the bride feeds the groom. This tradition makes beautiful wedding photographs.

You will need toasting glasses to toast each other after cutting the cake. They are usually decorated with ribbons or flowers and kept near the cake. This tradition also makes beautiful wedding photographs.

Things to Consider: Consider having your initials and wedding date engraved on your wedding knife as a memento. Consider purchasing crystal or silver toasting glasses as a keepsake of your wedding. Have your florist decorate your knife and toasting glasses with flowers or ribbons.

GREEN WEDDING TIP

Rent a Cake
A lavish wedding cake is part of any bride's dream, but their production and delivery are expensive and not always eco-friendly. Have your cake and eat it too by renting a fake wedding cake! RenttheCakeof YourDreams.com makes realistic-looking fake cakes you can rent for a fraction of the price. These fakes even contain a space for actual cake so you can still have a traditional cake cutting. Afterwards, the fake is whisked away and your caterer will serve a sheet cake that's been cut behind the scenes. Renting a cake is an unusual but eco-friendly way to reduce waste without sacrificing style.

Tips to Save Money: Borrow your cake knife or toasting glasses from a friend or family member as "something borrowed," an age-old wedding tradition. Use the reception facility's glasses and knife, and decorate them with flowers or ribbon.

Price Range: $15 - $120 for knife; $10 - $100 for toasting glasses

BAKERY COMPARISON CHART

Questions	POSSIBILITY 1
What is the name of the bakery?	
What is the bakery's website and e-mail?	
What is the address of the bakery?	
What is the name and phone number of my contact person?	
How long have you been in business?	
What are your wedding cake specialties?	
Do you offer free tasting of your wedding cakes?	
Are your wedding cakes fresh or frozen?	
How far in advance should I order my cake?	
Can you make a groom's cake?	
Do you lend, rent, or sell cake knives?	
What is the cost per serving of my desired cake?	
What is your cake pillar and plate rental fee?	
Is this fee refundable upon the return of these items?	
When must these items be returned?	
What is your cake delivery and setup fee?	
What is your payment/cancellation policy?	

POSSIBILITY 2	POSSIBILITY 3

WEDDING PLANNING NOTES

Flowers

FLOWERS ADD BEAUTY, FRAGRANCE, AND COLOR to your wedding. Like everything else, flowers should fit your overall style and color scheme. The purpose of flowers at the main altar is to direct the guests' visual attention toward the front of the church and to the bridal couple. Therefore, they must be seen by guests seated toward the back. You may also want to use flowers or ribbons to mark the aisle pews and add color.

BRIDE'S BOUQUET

The bridal bouquet is one of the most important elements of the bride's attire and deserves special attention. Start by selecting the color and shape of the bouquet. The bridal bouquet should be carried low enough so that all the intricate details of your gown are visible.

Options: There are many colors, scents, sizes, shapes, and styles of bouquets to choose from. Popular styles are the cascade, cluster, contemporary, and hand-tied garden bouquets. The traditional bridal bouquet is made of white flowers. Stephanotis, gardenias, white roses, orchids, and lilies of the valley are popular choices for an all-white bouquet.

If you prefer a colorful bouquet, you may want to consider using roses, tulips, stock, peonies, freesia, and gerbera, which come in a wide variety of colors. Using scented flowers in your bouquet will evoke memories of your wedding day whenever you smell them in the future. Popular fragrant flowers are gardenias, freesia, stephanotis, bouvardia, and narcissus. Select flowers that are in season to assure availability.

Things to Consider: Your flowers should complement the season, your gown, your color scheme, your attendants' attire, and the style and formality of your wedding. If you have a favorite flower, build your bouquet around it and include it in all your arrangements. Some flowers carry centuries of symbolism. Consider stephanotis— tradition regards it as the bridal good-luck flower! Pimpernel signifies change; white flowers radiate innocence; forget-me-nots indicate true love; and ivy stands for friendship, fidelity, and matrimony—the three essentials for a happy marriage.

No flower, however, has as much symbolism for brides as the orange blossom, having at least 700 years of nuptial history. Its unusual ability to simultaneously bear flowers and produce fruit symbolizes the fusion of beauty, personality, and fertility.

Whatever flowers you select, final arrangements should be made well in advance of your wedding date to insure availability. Confirm your final order and delivery time a few days before the wedding. Have the flowers delivered before the photographer arrives so that you can include them in your pre-ceremony photos.

In determining the size of your bouquet, consider your gown and your overall stature. Carry a smaller bouquet if you're petite or if your gown is fairly ornate. A long, cascading bouquet complements a fairly simple gown or a tall or larger bride. Arm bouquets look best when resting naturally in the crook of your arm. For a natural, fresh-picked look, have your florist put together a cluster of flowers tied together with a ribbon. For a Victorian appeal, carry a nosegay or a basket filled with flowers. Or carry a Bible or other family heirloom decorated with just a few flowers. For a contemporary look, you may want to consider carrying an arrangement of calla lilies or other long-stemmed flower over your arm. For a dramatic statement, carry a single stem of your favorite flower!

Beware: If your bouquet includes delicate flowers that will not withstand hours of heat or a lack of water, make sure your florist uses a bouquet holder to keep them fresh. If you want to carry fresh-cut stems without a bouquet holder, make sure the flowers you select are hardy enough to go without water for the duration of your ceremony and reception.

Tips to Save Money: The cost of some flowers may be significantly higher during their off season. Try to select flowers that are in bloom and plentiful at the time of your wedding. Avoid exotic, out-of-season flowers. Allow your florist to emphasize your colors using more reasonable, seasonal flowers to achieve your overall look. If you have a favorite flower that is costly or out of season, consider using silk for that one flower.

Avoid scheduling your wedding on holidays such as Valentine's Day and Mother's Day when the price of flowers is higher. Because every attendant will carry or wear flowers, consider keeping the size of your wedding party down to accommodate your floral budget.

Price Range: $75 - $400

TOSSING BOUQUET

If you want to preserve your bridal bouquet, consider having your florist make a smaller, less expensive bouquet specifically for tossing. This will be the bouquet you toss to your single, female friends toward the end of the reception. Tradition has it that the woman who catches the bouquet is the next to be married. Have your florist include a few sprigs of fresh ivy in the tossing bouquet to symbolize friendship and fidelity.

Tips to Save Money: Use the floral cake top or guest book table "tickler bouquet" as the tossing bouquet. Or omit the tossing bouquet altogether and simply toss your bridal bouquet.

GREEN WEDDING TIP

If You Buy Organic, Coordinate With Your Florist
Because organic flowers are not preserved in the same way conventionally grown flowers are, they don't last as long. Therefore, if you decide to go organic, your florist will need to be on top of ordering, delivery, and arrangement schedules so you don't end up with wilted or browning flowers. Also, if your florist is unfamiliar with working with organics, let him or her know to look either for the USDA Certified Organics emblem or the VeriFlora seal (the first green certification standard for the floral industry).

Price Range: $20 - $100

MAID OF HONOR'S BOUQUET

The maid of honor's bouquet can be somewhat larger or of a different color than the rest of the bridesmaids' bouquets. This will help to set her apart from the others.

Price Range: $25 - $100

BRIDESMAIDS' BOUQUETS

The bridesmaids' bouquets should complement the bridal bouquet, but are generally smaller in size. The size and color should coordinate with the bridesmaids' dresses and the overall style of the wedding. Bridesmaids' bouquets are usually identical.

Options: To personalize your bridesmaids' bouquets, insert a different flower in each of their bouquets to make a statement. For example, if one of your bridesmaids has been sad, give her a lily of the valley to symbolize the return of happiness. To tell a friend that you admire her, insert yellow jasmine. A pansy will let your friend know that you are thinking of her.

Things to Consider: Choose a bouquet style (cascade, cluster, contemporary, hand-tied) that complements the formality of your wedding and the height of your attendants. If your bridesmaids will be wearing floral print dresses, select flowers that complement the floral print.

Tips to Save Money: Have your attendants carry a single stemmed rose, lily, or other suitable flower for an elegant look that also saves money.

Price Range: $25 - $100

MAID OF HONOR/BRIDESMAIDS' HAIRPIECE

For a garden look, have your maid of honor and bridesmaids wear garlands of flowers in their hair. If so, provide your maid of honor with a slightly different color or variety of flower to set her apart from the others.

Options: You may consider using artificial flowers for the hairpieces as long as they are in keeping with the flowers carried by members of the bridal party. Since it is not always easy to find good artificial blooms, other types of hairpieces may be more satisfactory, durable, and attractive.

Things to Consider: Flowers in the hairpiece must be hardy and long-lived.

Price Range: $8 - $100

FLOWER GIRL'S HAIRPIECE

Flower girls often wear a wreath of flowers as a hairpiece.

Options: This is another place where artificial flowers may be used, but they must be in keeping with the flowers carried by members of the bridal party. Since it is not always easy to find good artificial blooms, other types of hairpieces may be more satisfactory, durable, and attractive.

Things to Consider: If the flowers used for the hairpiece are not a sturdy and long-lived variety, a ribbon, bow, or hat might be a safer choice.

Price Range: $8 - $75

 GREEN WEDDING TIP

Decorate Seasonally
Demanding tulips at your February wedding is going to cost both you and the environment. As with your menu, decorating your wedding with seasonally available plants and flowers saves money and is easier on the earth. And you still have many luxurious options at your fingertips! Winter weddings can be festively decorated with cranberries, pine cones, lemon leaf garlands, and sprigs of holly and mistletoe. Likewise, autumn weddings can feature a rich array of golds, browns, and oranges, and floral arrangements might include small decorative pumpkins, pomegranates, artichokes, and leaves.

BRIDE'S GOING AWAY CORSAGE

You may want to consider wearing a corsage on your going away outfit. This makes for pretty photos as you and your new husband leave the reception for your honeymoon. Have your florist create a corsage that echoes the beauty of your bouquet.

Beware: Put a protective shield under lilies when using them as a corsage, as their anthers will stain fabric. Be careful when using alstroemeria as a corsage, as its sap can be harmful if it enters the bloodstream.

Tips to Save Money: Ask your florist if he or she can design your bridal bouquet in such a way that the center flowers may be removed and worn as a corsage. Or omit this corsage altogether.

Price Range: $10 - $50

FAMILY MEMBERS' CORSAGES

The groom is responsible for providing flowers for his mother, the bride's mother, and the grandmothers. The officiant, if female, may also be given a corsage to reflect her important role in the ceremony. The corsages don't have to be identical, but they should be coordinated with the color of their dresses.

GREEN WEDDING TIP

A Flower's After Party
The flowers that bring romance to a wedding often end up in the trash by the time the couple reaches the honeymoon suite. Instead of sending them to the landfill, have your flowers composted after the wedding. Or, have them dried and turned into decorative potpourri bags (if these are small enough, include them with the thank you cards you send to your guests). Finally, donate your flowers to a local institution that may need brightening up, such as a hospital, funeral home, or elderly care center.

Options: The groom may order flowers that can be pinned to a pocketbook or worn around a wrist. He should ask which style the women prefer, and if a particular color is needed to coordinate with their dresses. Gardenias, camellias, white orchids, or cymbidium orchids are excellent choices for corsages, as they go well with any outfit.

Things to Consider: The groom may also want to consider ordering corsages for other close family members, such as sisters and aunts. This will add a little to your floral expenses but will make these female family members feel more included in your wedding and will let guests know that they are related to the bride and groom. Many women do not like to wear corsages, so the groom should check with the people involved before ordering the flowers.

Beware: Put a protective shield under lilies when using them as corsages, as their anthers will easily stain fabric. Be careful when using alstroemeria as corsages, as its sap can be harmful if it enters the human bloodstream.

Tips to Save Money: Ask your florist to recommend reasonable flowers for corsages. Dendrobium orchids are reasonable and make lovely corsages.

Price Range: $10 - $35

GREEN WEDDING TIP

One Set of Flowers Can Serve Two Weddings
Caring about the environment means going out of your way to reduce, reuse, and recycle. With this mantra in mind, consider sharing your flowers with another couple getting married the same day. If you've booked your wedding in a ballroom, hotel, restaurant, or historical property, chances are someone is getting married either just before or just after you. Get this couple's name, and talk with them about their color scheme and preferences. It may be possible to split the financial and environmental costs that flowers incur.

GROOM'S BOUTONNIERE

The groom wears his boutonniere on the left lapel, nearest to his heart.

Options: Boutonnieres are generally a single blossom such as a rosebud, stephanotis, freesia, or a miniature carnation. If a rosebud is used for the wedding party, have the groom wear two rosebuds, or add a sprig of baby's breath to differentiate him from the groomsmen.

Things to Consider: You may use a small cluster of flowers instead of a single bloom for the groom's boutonniere.

Beware: Be careful when using alstroemeria as a boutonniere, as its sap can be harmful if it enters the human bloodstream.

Tips to Save Money: Use mini-carnations rather than roses.

Price Range: $4 - $25

GREEN WEDDING TIP

Save the Oasis for Your Honeymoon

Organic flowers? Check. Dried or reusable arrangement accessories? Check. The only thing left for a totally eco-friendly floral arrangement is to avoid using oasis—the green foam brick florists soak in water and use to showcase arrangements. Oasis is made from plastic and is not biodegradable, so ask your florist to work with something less toxic. For example, hold flowers together with vines that are wrapped tightly around flower stems. These become part of the arrangement design and can be dried or composted with the flowers after the wedding.

USHERS/OTHER FAMILY MEMBERS' BOUTONNIERES

The groom gives each man in his wedding party a boutonniere to wear on his left lapel. The officiant, if male, may also be given a boutonniere to reflect his important role in the ceremony. The ring bearer may or may not wear a boutonniere, depending on his outfit. A boutonniere is more appropriate on a tuxedo than on knickers and knee socks.

Options: Generally, a single blossom such as a rosebud, freesia, or miniature carnation is used as a boutonniere.

Things to Consider: The groom should also consider ordering boutonnieres for other close family members such as fathers, grandfathers, and brothers. This will add a little to your floral expenses, but will make these male family members feel more included in your wedding and will let guests know that they are related to the bride and groom.

Tips to Save Money: Use mini-carnations rather than roses.

Price Range: $3 - $15

MAIN ALTAR

The purpose of flowers at the main altar is to direct the guests' visual attention toward the front of the church or synagogue and to the bridal couple. Therefore, they must be seen by guests seated in the back. The flowers for the ceremony site can be as elaborate or as simple as you wish. Your officiant's advice, or that of the altar guild or florist, can be most helpful in choosing flowers for the altar.

Options: If your ceremony is outside, decorate the arch, gazebo, or other structure serving as the altar with flowers or greenery. In a Jewish ceremony, vows are said under a Chuppah, which is placed at the altar and covered with greens and fresh flowers.

Things to Consider: In choosing floral accents, consider the decor of your ceremony site. Some churches and synagogues are ornate enough and don't need extra flowers. Too many arrangements would get lost in the architectural splendor. Select a few dramatic showpieces that will complement the existing decor. Be sure to ask if there are any restrictions on flowers at the church or synagogue. Remember, decorations should be determined by the size and style of the building, the formality of the wedding, the preferences of the bride, the cost, and the regulations of the particular site.

Tips to Save Money: Decorate the ceremony site with greenery only. Candlelight and greenery are elegant in and of themselves. Use greenery and flowers from your garden. Have your ceremony outside in a beautiful garden or by the water, surrounded by nature's own splendor.

Price Range: $50 - $3,000

ALTAR CANDELABRA

In a candlelight ceremony, the candelabra may be decorated with flowers or greens for a dramatic effect.

Options: Ivy may be twined around the candelabra, or flowers may be strung to them.

Price Range: $50 - $200

AISLE PEWS

Flowers, candles, or ribbons are often used to mark the aisle pews and add color.

 GREEN WEDDING TIP

Make Your Flowers Work a Double Shift
Whether you use cut flowers, potted plants, or flower alternatives, make sure your arrangements do double duty by being showcased in both your ceremony and reception. Depending on how far these are from each other, this can be tricky but worth it. Having one set of arrangements cuts down on both the cost and the amount needed (and thus wasted). Ask your wedding coordinator to work with your florist and caterer to move arrangements from ceremony to reception site during the cocktail hour when guests will be preoccupied.

Options: A cluster of flowers, a cascade of greens, or a cascade of flowers and ribbons are all popular choices. Candles with adorning greenery add an elegant touch.

Things to Consider: Use hardy flowers that can tolerate being handled as pew ornaments. Gardenias and camellias, for example, are too sensitive to last long.

Beware: Avoid using allium in your aisle pew decorations as they have an odor of onions.

Tips to Save Money: It is not necessary to decorate all of the aisle pews, or any at all. To save money, decorate only the reserved family pews. Or decorate every second or third pew.

Price Range: $5 - $75

RECEPTION SITE

Flowers add beauty, fragrance, and color to your reception. Flowers for the reception, like everything else, should fit your overall style and color scheme. Flowers can help transform a stark reception hall into a warm, inviting, and colorful room.

Things to Consider: You can rent indoor plants or small trees to give your reception a garden-like
atmosphere. Decorate them with twinkle lights to achieve a magical effect.

Tips to Save Money: You can save money by taking flowers from the ceremony to the reception site for decorations. However, you must coordinate this move carefully to avoid having your guests arrive at an undecorated reception room. Use greenery rather than flowers to fill large areas. Trees and garlands of ivy can give a dramatic impact for little money. Use greenery and flowers from your garden. Have your reception outside in a beautiful garden or by the water, surrounded by nature's own beauty.

Price Range: $300 - $3,000

HEAD TABLE

The head table is where the wedding party will sit during the reception. This important table should be decorated with a larger or more dramatic centerpiece than the guest tables.

Things to Consider: Consider using a different color or style of arrangement to set the head table apart from the other tables.

Beware: Avoid using highly fragrant flowers, such as narcissus, on tables where food is being served or eaten, as their fragrance may conflict with other aromas.

Tips to Save Money: Decorate the head table with the bridal and attendants' bouquets.

Price Range: $100 - $600

GUEST TABLES

At a reception where guests are seated, a small flower arrangement may be placed on each table.

Things to Consider: The arrangements should complement the table linens and the size of the table, and should be kept low enough so as not to hinder conversation among guests seated across from each other. Avoid using highly fragrant flowers, like narcissus, on tables where food is being served or eaten, as their fragrance may conflict with other aromas.

Tips to Save Money: To keep the cost down and for less formal receptions, use small potted flowering plants placed in white baskets, or consider using dried or silk arrangements that you can make yourself and give later as gifts. Or place a wreath of greenery entwined with colored ribbon in the center of each table. Use a different colored ribbon at each table and assign your guests to tables by ribbon color instead of number.

Price Range: $10 - $100

BUFFET TABLE

If buffet tables are used, have some type of floral arrangement on the tables to add color and beauty to your display of food.

Options: Whole fruits and bunches of berries offer a variety of design possibilities. Figs add a festive touch. Pineapples are a sign of hospitality. Vegetables offer an endless array of options to decorate with. Herbs are yet another option in decorating. A mixture of rosemary and mint combined with scented geraniums makes a very unique table decoration.

Things to Consider: Depending on the size of the table, place one or two arrangements at each side.

Beware: Avoid placing certain flowers, such as carnations, snapdragons, or the star of Bethlehem, next to buffet displays of fruits or vegetables, as they are extremely sensitive to the gasses emitted by these foods.

Price Range: $50 - $500

PUNCH TABLE

Put an assortment of greens or a small arrangement of flowers at the punch table. See "Buffet Table."

Price Range: $10 - $100

CAKE TABLE

The wedding cake is often the central location at the reception. Decorate the cake table with flowers.

Tips to Save Money: Have your bridesmaids place their bouquets on the cake table during the reception, or decorate the cake top only and surround the base with greenery and a few loose flowers.

Price Range: $30 - $300

CAKE

Flowers are a beautiful addition to a wedding cake and are commonly seen spilling out between the cake tiers.

Things to Consider: Use only nonpoisonous flowers, and have your florist—not the caterer—design the floral decorations for your cake. A florist will be able to blend the cake decorations into your overall floral theme.

Price Range: $20 - $100

CAKE KNIFE

Decorate your cake knife with a white satin ribbon and flowers.

Things to Consider: Consider engraving the cake knife with your names and wedding date.

Price Range: $5 - $35

TOASTING GLASSES

Tie small flowers with white ribbon onto the stems of your champagne glasses. These wedding accessories deserve a special floral touch since they will most likely be included in your special photographs.

Things to Consider: Consider engraving your toasting glasses with your names and wedding date.

Price Range: $10 - $35

FLORAL DELIVERY/SETUP

Most florists charge a fee to deliver flowers to the ceremony and reception sites and to arrange them on site.

Things to Consider: Make sure your florist knows where your sites are and what time to arrive for setup.

Price Range: $25 - $200

FLOWER	Winter	Spring	Summer	Fall
Allium		X	X	
Alstroemeria	X	X	X	X
Amaryllis	X		X	
Anemone	X	X		X
Aster	X	X	X	X
Baby's Breath	X	X	X	X
Bachelor's Button	X	X	X	X
Billy Buttons		X	X	
Bird of Paradise	X	X	X	X
Bouvardia	X	X	X	X
Calla Lily	X	X	X	X
Carnation	X	X	X	X
Celosia		X	X	
Chrysanthemum	X	X	X	X
Daffodils		X		
Dahlia			X	X
Delphinium			X	X
Eucalyptus	X	X	X	X
Freesia	X	X	X	X
Gardenia	X	X	X	X
Gerbera	X	X	X	X
Gladiolus	X	X	X	X
Iris	X	X	X	X
Liatris	X	X	X	X
Lily	X	X	X	X

FLOWERS AND THEIR SEASONS

FLOWER	Winter	Spring	Summer	Fall
Lily of the Valley		X		
Lisianthus		X	X	X
Narcissus	X	X		X
Nerine	X	X	X	X
Orchid (Cattleya)	X	X	X	X
Orchid (Cymbidium)	X	X	X	X
Peony		X		
Pincushion			X	
Protea	X			X
Queen Anne's Lace			X	
Ranunculas		X		
Rose	X	X	X	X
Saponaria			X	
Snapdragon		X	X	X
Speedwell			X	
Star of Bethlehem	X			X
Statice	X	X	X	X
Stephanotis	X	X	X	X
Stock	X	X	X	X
Sunflower		X	X	X
Sweet Pea		X		
Tuberose			X	X
Tulip	X	X		
Waxflower	X	X		

Bride's Bouquet

Color Scheme: _____

Style: _____

Flowers: _____

_____

_____

Greenery: _____

Other (Ribbons, etc.): _____

Maid of Honor's Bouquet

Color Scheme: _____

Style: _____

Flowers: _____

_____

Greenery: _____

Other (Ribbons, etc.): _____

Bridesmaids' Bouquet

Color Scheme: _____

Style: _____

Flowers: _____

_____

Greenery: _____

Other (Ribbons, etc.): _____

BOUQUETS AND FLOWERS

Flower Girls' Bouquet

Color Scheme: _____

Style: _____

Flowers: _____

_____

_____

Greenery: _____

Other (Ribbons, etc.): _____

_____

_____

Other

Groom's Boutonniere: _____

_____

Ushers' and Other Family Members' Boutonnieres: _____

_____

Mother of the Bride Corsage: _____

_____

Mother of the Groom Corsage: _____

_____

Altar or Chuppah: _____

_____

Steps to Altar or Chuppah: _____

_____

_____

Other

Pews:

_____

_____

Entrance to the Ceremony:

_____

_____

Entrance to the Reception:

_____

_____

Receiving Line:

_____

_____

Head Table:

_____

_____

Parents' Table:

_____

_____

Guest Table:

_____

_____

Cake Table:

_____

_____

Serving Table (Buffet, Dessert):

_____

_____

Gift Table:

_____

_____

FLORIST COMPARISON CHART

Questions	POSSIBILITY 1
What is the name of the florist?	
What is the website and e-mail of the florist?	
What is the address of the florist?	
What are your business hours?	
What is the name and phone number of my contact person?	
How many years of professional floral experience do you have?	
What percentage of your business is dedicated to weddings?	
Do you have access to out-of-season flowers?	
Will you visit my wedding sites to make floral recommendations?	
Can you preserve my bridal bouquet?	
Do you rent vases and candleholders?	
Can you provide silk flowers?	
What is the cost of the desired bridal bouquet?	
What is the cost of the desired boutonniere/corsage?	
Do you have liability insurance?	
What are your delivery/setup fees?	
What is your payment/cancellation policy?	

POSSIBILITY 2	POSSIBILITY 3

WEDDING PLANNING NOTES

Decorations

DECORATIONS CAN ENHANCE YOUR WEDDING by unifying all of the components of your ceremony and reception. Decorations can range anywhere from floral arrangements, twinkling lights, and centerpieces to more personal touches such as seating cards, menus, favors, and more.

Decorations, from centerpieces to place settings, usually fall under a unified theme. For example, paper lanterns and take-out boxes can create beautiful Asian-inspired style. Or, consider decorations that represent you as a couple; for instance, a pair of writers might decorate with vintage books and an antique typewriter. It's completely up to you!

TABLE CENTERPIECES

Each of the tables at your reception, including the head table, should be decorated with a centerpiece.

Options: Candles, mirrors, water centerpieces and flowers are popular choices for table centerpieces. However, the options are endless. Just be creative!

 GREEN WEDDING TIP

Make Centerpieces Out of Reusable Items
Your wedding can be made more earth-friendly by making your centerpieces out of items that will have a life beyond the party. Build centerpieces from materials you are sure to reuse, such as ribbon, fabric, paper lanterns, baskets, pots, glass bowls, and candleholders. Make personalized centerpieces out of framed pictures of your guests or images from your life with your partner that you can later use as décor around your home. Invite your guests to pilfer the centerpieces and take what they think they will use.

Use Eco-Friendly Candles
Using candles cuts down on the electricity used to light up your wedding. When selecting candles, avoid cheap, environmentally hazardous ones made from paraffin-based wax, which is a petroleum by-product. Also skip artificially scented candles—these often have wicks that release chemicals into the air. Instead, choose cotton-wicked candles made from soy, beeswax, or vegetable-based oils. These materials are renewable, sustainable, biodegradable, water soluble, and non-toxic. Plus, they last longer than wax candles since they burn at lower temperatures.

An arrangement of shells, for example, makes a very nice centerpiece for a seaside reception. Floating candles in a low, round bowl make a romantic centerpiece for an evening reception.

Things to Consider: Select table centerpieces that complement your colors and setting.

Make sure that your centerpieces at each table are kept low enough so as not to hinder conversation among guests seated across from each other.

Consider using a centerpiece that your guests can take home as a memento of your wedding.

Tips to Save Money: Shop at antique stores and on eBay for vintage pieces like mason jars, milk crates, vases, and glass bowls, which can be filled with flowers, stones, or buttons for inexpensive, pretty centerpieces.

Non-floral items also make for a less-expensive option. Stones, fruit, shells, and succulents make for a unique look.

Price Range: $10 - $100 each

TABLE NUMBERS

You should think about how to differentiate your guest tables, either with traditional table numbers or an overarching theme.

Options: Tables can simply be numbered. Jazz up your table numbers with photos of you as a couple on each table. Or, consider personalizing each table with a theme special and unique to you as a couple. For instance, name each table after cities you have visited together or after your favorite movies.

Price Range: $1 - $10 each

Transportation

IT IS CUSTOMARY FOR THE BRIDE and her father to ride to the ceremony site together on the wedding day. You may also include some or all members of your wedding party.

Normally a procession to the church begins with the bride's mother and several of the bride's attendants in the first vehicle.

If desired, you can provide a second vehicle for the rest of the attendants. The bride and her father will go in the last vehicle. This vehicle will also be used to transport the bride and groom to the reception site after the ceremony.

TRANSPORTATION

Options: There are various options for transportation. The most popular choice is a limousine, since it is large and open and

GREEN WEDDING TIP

Get Your Guests Together
The average wedding has around 140 to 150 guests. Assuming most guests come in pairs, around 70 cars will be driving first to your ceremony site and then to your reception. To cut down on the CO_2 your guests release as they share in your special day, consider renting a bus to get them from place to place. It cuts down on pollution, and you won't have to print individual driving directions or worry anyone will be late to the party. Or, hold your ceremony and reception in the same place.

can accommodate several people, as well as your bridal gown. If you would like to ride with your entire wedding party, consider riding in style in a trendy stretch-Hummer limo.

You can also choose to rent a car that symbolizes your personality as a couple. You might rent a luxury car such as a Mercedes, sports cars such as a Ferrari, or a vintage vehicle such as a 1950s Thunderbird or 1930s Cadillac.

If your ceremony and reception sites are fairly close together, and if weather permits, you might want to consider a horse-drawn carriage. This is a very elegant and special way to arrive in style; however, you should check with the venue to make sure their location can accommodate the carriage. For instance, if you are getting married in a big city, it may be a traffic obstruction to have a carriage.

Things to Consider: In some areas of the country, limousines are booked on a three-hour-minimum basis.

Always make sure the company you choose is fully licensed and has liability insurance. Do not pay the full amount until after the event.

Tips to Save Money: Consider hiring only one large limousine. This limousine can transport you, your parents, and your attendants to the ceremony, and then you and your new husband from the ceremony to the reception.

Price Range: $35 - $100 per hour

TO CEREMONY SITE

Passenger	Pickup Time	Pickup Location	Vehicle/Driver
Bride			
Groom			
Bride's Parents			
Groom's Parents			
Bridesmaids			
Ushers			
Other:			
Other:			
Other:			

TO RECEPTION SITE

Passenger	Pickup Time	Pickup Location	Vehicle/Driver
Bride and Groom			
Bride's Parents			
Groom's Parents			
Bridesmaids			
Ushers			
Other:			
Other:			

TRANSPORTATION COMPARISON CHART

Questions	POSSIBILITY 1
What is the name of the transportation service?	
What is the website and e-mail of the transportation service?	
What is the address of the transportation service?	
What is the name and phone number of my contact person?	
How many years have you been in business?	
How many vehicles and drivers do you have available?	
Can you provide a back-up vehicle in case of an emergency?	
What types of vehicles are available?	
What are the various sizes of vehicles available?	
How old are the vehicles?	
Can you show me photos of your drivers?	
How do your drivers dress for weddings?	
Do you have liability insurance?	
What is the minimum amount of time required to rent a vehicle?	
What is the cost per hour? Two hours? Three hours?	
How much gratuity is expected?	
What is your payment/cancellation policy?	

POSSIBILITY 2	POSSIBILITY 3

WEDDING PLANNING NOTES

Rental Items

RENTALS ALLOW YOU TO HOST A RECEPTION
in your own home or in less traditional
locations, such as an art museum, a local
park, or at the beach. Be sure to take into
account the cost for all these rental items
when creating your budget.

CEREMONY ACCESSORIES

Ceremony rental accessories are the additional items needed for the ceremony but not included in the ceremony site fee.

Options: Ceremony rental accessories may include the following items:

Aisle Runner: A thin rug made of plastic, paper or cloth extending the length of the aisle. It is rolled out after the mothers are seated, just prior to the processional. Plastic or paper doesn't work well on grass; but if you must use one of these types of runners, make sure the grass is clipped short.

Kneeling Cushion: A small cushion or pillow placed in front of the altar where the bride and groom kneel for their wedding blessing.

Arch (Christian): A white lattice or brass arch where the bride and groom exchange their vows, often decorated with flowers and greenery.

Chuppah (Jewish): A canopy under which a Jewish ceremony is performed, symbolizing cohabitation and consummation.

You may also need to consider renting audio equipment, aisle stanchions, candelabra, candles, candle-lighters, chairs, heaters, a gift table, a guest book stand, and a canopy.

Things to Consider: Make sure the rental supplier has been in business for a good amount of time and has a good reputation. Reserve the items you need well in advance. Find out the company's payment, reservation, and cancellation policies.

Some companies allow you to reserve emergency items, such as heaters or canopies, without having to pay for them unless needed, in which case you would need to call the rental company a day or two in advance to request the items. If someone else requests the items you have reserved, the company should give you the right of first refusal.

Tips to Save Money: When considering a ceremony outside of a church, figure the cost of rental items. Negotiate a package deal, if possible, by renting items for both the ceremony and the reception from the same supplier. Consider renting these items from your florist so you only have to pay one delivery fee.

Price Range: $100 - $500

TENT/CANOPY

A large tent or canopy may be required for receptions held outdoors to protect you and your guests from the sun or rain. Tents and canopies can be expensive due to the labor involved in delivery and setup.

Options: Tents and canopies come in different sizes and colors. Depending on the shape of your reception area, you may need to rent several smaller canopies rather than one large one. Contact several party rental suppliers to discuss the options.

Things to Consider: Consider this cost when making a decision between an outdoor and an indoor reception. In cooler weather, heaters may also be necessary.

Tips to Save Money: Shop early and compare prices with several party rental suppliers. Also, if there is another couple hosting a wedding at your same venue during the same weekend, contact them about splitting the cost of a tent.

Price Range: $300 - $5,000

DANCE FLOOR

A dance floor will be provided by most hotels and clubs. However, if your reception site does not have a dance floor, you may need to rent one through your caterer or a party rental supplier.

Things to Consider: When comparing prices of dance floors, include the delivery and setup fees.

Price Range: $100 - $600

TABLES/CHAIRS

You will have to provide tables and chairs for your guests if your reception site or caterer doesn't provide them as part of their package. For a full meal, you will have to provide tables and seating for all guests. For a cocktail reception, you only need to provide tables and chairs for approximately 30 to 50 percent of your guests. Ask your caterer or reception site manager for advice.

Options: There are various types of tables and chairs to choose from. The most commonly used chairs for wedding receptions are typically white wooden or plastic chairs. The most common tables for receptions are round tables that seat eight guests. The most common head table arrangement is several rectangular tables placed end-to-end to seat your entire wedding party on one side, facing your guests. Contact various party rental suppliers to find out what types of chairs and tables they carry, as well as their price ranges.

Things to Consider: When comparing prices of renting tables and chairs, include the cost of delivery and setup.

Tips to Save Money: Attempt to negotiate free delivery and setup with party rental suppliers in exchange for giving them your business.

Price Range: $3 - $10 per person

LINENS/TABLEWARE

You will also need to provide linens and tableware for your reception if your reception site or caterer does not provide them as part of their package.

Options: For a sit-down reception where the meal is served by waiters and waitresses, tables are usually set with a cloth (usually white, but may be color coordinated with the wedding), a centerpiece, and complete place settings. At a less formal buffet reception where guests serve themselves, tables are covered with a cloth, but place settings are not mandatory. The necessary plates and silverware may be located at the buffet table, next to the food.

Things to Consider: Linens and tableware depend on the formality of your reception. When comparing prices of linens and tableware, include the cost of delivery and setup.

Price Range: $3 - $25 per person

HEATERS

You may need to rent heaters if your ceremony or reception will be held outdoors and if the temperature could drop below sixty-five degrees.

Options: There are electric and gas heaters, both of which come in different sizes. Gas heaters are more popular since they do not have unsightly and unsafe electric cords.

Price Range: $25 - $75 each

LANTERNS

Lanterns are often used at evening receptions to add soft lighting.

Options: Many choices are available, from fire lanterns to electric ones.

Price Range: $6 - $60

MISCELLANEOUS RENTAL ITEMS

If your reception site or caterer doesn't provide them, you will need to purchase, rent, or borrow other miscellaneous items for your reception, such as trash cans, a gift table, trash bags, and so on.

BRIDAL SLIP

The bridal slip is an undergarment that gives the bridal gown its proper shape.

Things to Consider: Be sure to wear the same slip you'll be wearing on your wedding day during your fittings. Many bridal salons rent slips. Schedule an appointment to pick up your slip one week before the wedding; otherwise, you run the risk of not having one available on your wedding day. If rented, the slip will have to be returned shortly after the wedding. Arrange for someone to do this for you within the allotted time.

Tips to Save Money: Rent a slip rather than purchasing one; chances are you will never use it again.

Price Range: $25 - $75

RENTAL SUPPLIER COMPARISON CHART

Questions	POSSIBILITY 1
What is the name of the party rental supplier?	
What is the address of the party rental supplier?	
What is the web site and e-mail of the party rental supplier?	
What is the name and phone number of my contact person?	
How many years have you been in business?	
What are your hours of operation?	
Do you have liability insurance?	
What is the cost per item needed?	
What is the cost of pickup and delivery?	
What is the cost of setting up the items rented?	
When would the items be delivered?	
When would the items be picked up after the event?	
What is your payment policy?	
What is your cancellation policy?	
Other:	
Other:	
Other:	

POSSIBILITY 2	POSSIBILITY 3

CEREMONY EQUIPMENT CHECKLIST

Rental Supplier: _____ Contact: _____

Website: _____

E-mail: _____

Address: _____

City: _____ State: _____ Zip: _____

Phone: _____ Hours: _____

Payment Policy: _____

Cancellation Policy: _____

Delivery Time: _____ Tear-Down Time: _____

Setup Time: _____ Pickup Time: _____

QTY.	ITEM	Description	Price	Total
	Arch/Altar		$	$
	Canopy (Chuppah)		$	$
	Backdrops		$	$
	Floor Candelabra		$	$
	Candles		$	$
	Candle lighters		$	$
	Kneeling Bench		$	$
	Aisle Stanchions		$	$
	Aisle Runners		$	$
	Guest Book Stand		$	$
	Gift Table		$	$
	Chairs		$	$
	Audio Equipment		$	$
	Lighting		$	$
	Heating/Cooling		$	$
	Umbrellas/Tents		$	$
	Bug Eliminator		$	$
	Coat/Hat Rack		$	$
	Garbage Cans		$	$

Rental Supplier: _____ Contact: _____

Website: _____

E-mail: _____

Address: _____

City: _____ State: _____ Zip: _____

Phone: _____ Hours: _____

Payment Policy: _____

Cancellation Policy: _____

Delivery Time: _____ Tear-Down Time: _____

Setup Time: _____ Pickup Time: _____

QTY.	ITEM	Description	Price	Total
	Audio Equipment		$	$
	Cake Table		$	$
	Candelabras/Candles		$	$
	Canopies		$	$
	Coat/Hat Rack		$	$
	Dance Floor		$	$
	Bug Eliminator		$	$
	Garbage Cans		$	$
	Gift Table		$	$
	Guest Tables		$	$
	Heating/Cooling		$	$
	High/Booster Chairs		$	$
	Lighting		$	$
	Mirror Disco Ball		$	$
	Place Card Table		$	$
	Tents		$	$
	Umbrellas		$	$
	Visual Equipment		$	$
	Wheelchair Ramp		$	$

WEDDING PLANNING NOTES

Gifts

GIFTS ARE A WONDERFUL WAY TO SHOW your appreciation to family, friends, members of your wedding party, and to all those who have assisted you in your wedding planning process. Brides and grooms usually like to exchange something small yet meaningful. Keepsake items make wonderful gifts for members of the wedding party.

BRIDE'S GIFT

The bride's gift is traditionally given by the groom to the bride. It is typically a personal gift, such as a piece of jewelry.

Options: A string of pearls, a watch, pearl earrings, jewelry box, perfume, or beautiful lingerie are nice gifts for the bride from her groom.

Things to Consider: This gift is not necessary and should be given only if your budget allows.

Tips to Save Money: Consider omitting this gift. A pretty card from the groom proclaiming his eternal love for the bride is a very special, yet inexpensive gift.

Price Range: $50 - $500

GROOM'S GIFT

The groom's gift is traditionally given by the bride to the groom.

Options: A watch, cufflinks, a set of golf clubs, electronics, or a beautiful album of boudoir photos are nice gifts for the groom from his bride.

Things to Consider: This gift is not necessary and should be given only if your budget allows.

Tips to Save Money: Consider omitting this gift. A pretty card from the bride proclaiming her eternal love for the groom is a very special, yet inexpensive gift.

Price Range: $50 - $500

BRIDESMAIDS' GIFTS

Bridesmaids' gifts are given by the bride to her bridesmaids and maid of honor as a permanent keepsake of the wedding.

Options: The perfect gift is jewelry or an accessory that can be worn both during and after the wedding. Choose earrings, a pashmina wrap, small clutch purse, or a hairpiece that complements your bridesmaids' dresses.

Other nice gift choices are a certificate for a spa treatment, personalized sweat suits or tank tops, favorite beauty products, a tote or cosmetic bag, and customized stationery.

Things to Consider: Bridesmaids' gifts are usually presented at the bridesmaids' luncheon, if there is one, or at the rehearsal dinner. The gift to the maid of honor may be similar to the bridesmaids' gifts, but should be a bit more expensive.

Tips to Save Money: Ask your photographer to take, at no extra charge, professional portraits of each bridesmaid and her escort for use as bridesmaids' gifts. Put the photos in pretty frames.

Price Range: $25 - $200 per gift

USHERS' GIFTS

Ushers' gifts are given by the groom to his ushers as a permanent keepsake of the wedding.

Options: For ushers' gifts consider something they can wear during and after the wedding, such as a watch or cufflinks.

Other great gifts include a leather wallet, money clip, cigars, a personalized flask, luxury shaving kit, or a bottle of fine wine.

Things to Consider: The groom should deliver his gifts to the ushers at the bachelor party or at the rehearsal dinner. The gift to the best man may be similar to the ushers' gifts, but should be a bit more expensive.

Tips to Save Money: Negotiate with your photographer to take, at no extra charge, professional portraits of each usher and his escort for use as ushers' gifts. Select a beautiful background that will remind your ushers of the occasion, such as your cake table.

Price Range: $25 - $200 per gift

WEDDING PLANNING NOTES

Parties

WEDDINGS ARE OFTEN MUCH MORE THAN A daylong celebration. There can be plenty of festivities before and even after the wedding day. Typically, the events that take place before a wedding include the engagement party, bridal shower, bachelor and bachelorette parties, bridesmaids' luncheon, and rehearsal dinner. Some couples also like to have a brunch the day after the wedding to relax and relive the previous evening's celebration.

ENGAGEMENT PARTY

The engagement party is generally thrown by the bride's family to celebrate the big news. Gifts are not required at this party.

Options: An engagement party is typically held in your parents' home; however, renting a space or having dinner in a nice restaurant are also acceptable.

Things to Consider: If your schedule won't allow for it, an engagement party is by no means a requirement.

BRIDAL SHOWER

Traditionally, your wedding shower is thrown by your maid of honor and bridesmaids, unless they are a member of your immediate family. Because a shower is a gift-giving occasion, it is not considered socially acceptable for anyone in your immediate family to host this event. If your mother or sisters wish to be involved, have them offer to help with the cost of the event or offer their home for it. The agenda usually includes some games and gift-opening. Be sure to have someone keep track of which gift is from whom.

Options: Tea parties, spa days, cocktail parties, and traditional at-home events are all options—these days even men are being invited as coed showers become more and more popular! Generally, an event is themed (lingerie, cooking, home decor), and the invitation should give guests an idea of what type of gift to bring.

Things to Consider: You may have several showers thrown for you. When creating your guest lists, be sure not to invite the same people to multiple showers (the exception being members of the wedding party, who may be invited to all showers without the obligation of bringing a gift.) Only include people who have been invited to the wedding—the only exception to this is a work shower, to which all coworkers may be invited, whether or not they are attending the wedding.

BACHELOR PARTY

The bachelor party is a male-only affair typically organized by the best man. He is responsible for selecting the date and reserving the place and entertainment as well as inviting the groom's male friends and family. The ushers should also help with the organization of this party.

Options: A bachelor party can be as simple as a group of guys getting together for dinner and drinks, a day of golfing, a casino daytrip, or a cruise. You might also attend a sporting event, brewery tour or tasting, or be adventurous and go skydiving or camping.

Things to Consider: You often hear wild stories about bachelor parties being nights full of women and alcohol, however, these types of events are actually quite rare. The bachelor party is simply a night for great friends and family to celebrate together. Make this party a memorable one. Make sure you do something different, and enjoy it!

Beware: Your best man should not plan your bachelor party for the night before the wedding, since chances are that you will consume a fair amount of alcohol and stay up late. You don't want to have a hangover or be exhausted during your wedding. It is much more appropriate to have the bachelor party two or three nights before the wedding. Tell your best man that you will be busy the night before the wedding, just in case he is planning to surprise you.

Your best man should designate a driver for you and for those who will be drinking alcohol. Remember, you and your best man are responsible for the well-being of everybody invited to the party.

BACHELORETTE PARTY

The bachelorette party is typically organized by the maid of honor for the females in the wedding party.

Options: The bachelorette party is a night for girlfriends and close family to celebrate together. Go out for dinner and drinks, have a spa day, go wine tasting, or on a day-cruise. Other fun options include a yoga or Pilates retreat, scavenger hunt, or a sporting event.

Things to Consider: The maid of honor should ask the bride what kind of party she wants — wild or mild. She should not plan the party for the night before the wedding, as you don't want to have a hangover or be exhausted during your wedding. A few weeks before or another date when the whole party can get together is more appropriate for the bachelorette party. You should also coordinate transportation for guests who are drinking.

The maid of honor should consider buying something funny or unique for the bride to wear to make her stand out, such as a feather boa, tiara, or beads.

BRIDESMAIDS' LUNCHEON

The bridesmaids' luncheon is given by the bride for her bridesmaids. It is not a shower; rather, it is simply a time for good friends to get together formally before the bride changes her status from single to married.

Things to Consider: You can give your bridesmaids their gifts at this gathering. Otherwise, plan to give them their gifts at the rehearsal dinner.

Price Range: $12 - $60 per person

REHEARSAL DINNER

It is customary that the groom's parents host a dinner party following the rehearsal, the evening before the wedding. The dinner usually includes the bridal party, their spouses or guests, both sets of parents, close family members, the officiant, and the wedding consultant and/or coordinator.

Options: The rehearsal dinner party can be held just about anywhere, from a restaurant, hotel, or private hall to the groom's parents' home.

Tips to Save Money: Restaurants specializing in Mexican food or pizza are fun yet inexpensive options.

Price Range: $10 - $100 per person

DAY-AFTER WEDDING BRUNCH

Many times, the newlyweds will want to host a brunch the day after the wedding to spend one last bit of time with their guests and to thank them for coming to the wedding. Brunch can be much less formal than the rest of the wedding.

Options: You can have your caterer provide food for this event. Or, enlist family members to help cook or pick up brunch foods. A family member who still wants to contribute to your wedding is a perfect choice to host. If many guests are at one hotel, consider having the brunch there. If the hotel offers a continental breakfast, ask the hotel to reserve space in the breakfast room for your group.

Things to Consider: The brunch need not be elaborate. Keep the menu simple and have bagels, croissants, jams, fruit, coffee, and juice.

Choose a reasonable time for the brunch: Not too early, as many guests will be recovering from the festivities of the reception, but not too late, as out-of-town guests will have travel arrangements to attend to.

Price Range: $10 - $25 per person

Miscellaneous

WITH ALL THAT IS INVOLVED IN PLANNING
a wedding it is easy to forget some simple but
necessary tasks. Be sure that you don't forget to
consider or complete some of the following items.

MARRIAGE LICENSE

Marriage license requirements are state-regulated and may be obtained from the County Clerk in most county courthouses.

Options: Some states (California and Nevada, for example) offer two types of marriage licenses: a public license and a confidential one. The public license is the most common one and requires a health certificate and a blood test. It can only be obtained at the County Clerk's office.

The confidential license is usually less expensive and does not require a health certificate or blood test. If offered, it can usually be obtained from most Justices of the Peace. An oath must be taken in order to receive either license.

Things to Consider: Requirements vary from state to state, but generally include the following points:

1. Applying for and paying the fee for the marriage license. There is usually a waiting period before the license is valid and a limited time before it expires.

2. Meeting residency requirements for the state and/or county where the ceremony will take place.

3. Meeting the legal age requirements for both bride and groom or having parental consent.

4. Presenting any required identification, birth or baptismal certificates, marriage eligibility, or other documents.

5. Obtaining a medical examination and/or blood test for both the bride and groom to detect communicable diseases.

Price Range: $20 - $100

PRENUPTIAL AGREEMENT

A prenuptial agreement is a legal contract between the bride and groom itemizing the property each brings into the marriage and explaining how those properties will be divided in case of divorce or death. Although you can write your own agreement, it is advisable to have an attorney draw up or review the document. The two of you should be represented by different attorneys.

Things to Consider: Consider a prenuptial agreement if one or both of you have a significant amount of capital or assets, or if there are children involved from a previous marriage. If you are going to live in a different state after the wedding, consider having an attorney from that state draw up or review your document.

Nobody likes to talk about divorce or death when planning a wedding, but it is very important to give these issues your utmost consideration. By drawing a prenuptial agreement, you encourage open communication and get a better idea of each other's needs and expectations. You should also consider drawing up or reviewing your wills at this time.

Tips to Save Money: Some software packages allow you to write your own will and prenuptial agreement, which can save you substantial attorney's fees. However, if you decide to draw either agreement on your own, you should still have an attorney review it.

Price Range: $500 - $3,000

BRIDAL GOWN PRESERVATION

The pride and joy you will experience in seeing your daughter and/or granddaughter wear your wedding gown on her wedding day will more than justify the expense of having your gown preserved. Bring your gown to a reputable dry cleaning company which specializes in preserving wedding gowns. They will dry clean your dress, vacuum seal it, and place it in an attractive box. By doing this, your gown will be protected from yellowing, falling apart, or getting damaged over the years. Most boxes have a plastic see-through window where you can show the top part of your dress to friends and family members without having to open the vacuum-sealed container.

Tips to Save Money: Some bridal boutiques offer gown preservation. Try to negotiate having your gown preserved for free with the purchase of a wedding gown. It's well worth the try! But remember, get any agreement in writing and be sure to have it signed by either the owner or the manager of the boutique.

Price Range: $100 - $250

BRIDAL BOUQUET PRESERVATION

The bridal bouquet can be preserved to make a beautiful memento of the wedding.

Things to Consider: Have your bouquet dried, mounted, and framed to hang on your wall or to display on an easel in a quiet corner of your home. You can also have an artist paint your bouquet.

Price Range: $100 - $500

WEDDING CONSULTANT

Wedding consultants are professionals whose training, expertise, and contacts will help make your wedding as close to perfect as it can possibly be. They can save you considerable time, money, and stress when planning your wedding. Wedding consultants have information on many ceremony and reception sites as well as reliable service providers, such as photographers, videographers, and florists, which will save you hours of investigation and legwork.

Wedding consultants can provide facilities and service providers to match your budget. They can also save you stress by ensuring that what you are planning is correct and that the service providers you hire are reliable and professional. Most service providers recommended by wedding consultants will go out of their way to do an excellent job for you so that the wedding consultant will continue to recommend their services.

Options: You can have a wedding consultant help you do as much or as little as you think necessary. A consultant can help you plan the whole event from the beginning to the end, helping you formulate a budget, and select your ceremony and reception site, flowers, wedding gown, invitations, and service providers. A wedding consultant can also help you at the end by coordinating the rehearsal and the wedding day. Remember, you want to feel like a guest at your own wedding. You and your family should not have to worry about any details on that special day. This is the wedding consultant's job!

Things to Consider: Strongly consider engaging the services of a wedding consultant. Contrary to what many people believe, a wedding consultant is part of your wedding budget, not an extra expense! A good wedding consultant should be able to save you at least the amount of his or her fee by suggesting less expensive alternatives that still enhance your wedding. In addition, many consultants obtain discounts from the service providers they work with. If this is not enough, they are more than worth their fee by serving as an intermediary between you and your parents and/or service providers.

When hiring a wedding consultant, make sure you check his or her references. Ask the consultant if he or she is a member of the Association of Bridal Consultants (ABC) and ask to see a current membership certificate. All ABC members agree to uphold a Code of Ethics and Standards of Membership. Many consultants have formal training and experience in event planning and in other specialties related to weddings, such as flower arranging and catering.

Price Range: $500 - $10,000

WEDDING PLANNING ONLINE

With a computer and an internet connection, you can ease the process of planning your wedding. A good wedding planning website will help you create a budget, select your service providers, generate a guest list, address invitations and create a wedding timeline. It can also keep track of payments made, invitations sent, RSVPs, gifts received, and much more. You can even create your registry or design a personal web page or website all about your wedding!

Options: WS Publishing Group has a great wedding planning site that follows hand-in-hand with this book! Go to www.WeddingSolutions.com and plan your entire wedding with our online tools.

TAXES

Don't forget to figure in the cost of taxes on all taxable items you purchase for your wedding. Many people make a big mistake by not figuring out the taxes they will have to pay for their wedding expenses. For example, if you are planning a reception for 250 guests with an estimated cost of $60 per person for food and beverages, your pretax expenses would be $15,000. A sales tax of 7.5 percent would mean an additional expense of $1,125! Find out what the sales tax is in your area and which items are taxable and figure this expense into your overall budget.

WEDDING PLANNING NOTES

NAME AND ADDRESS CHANGE FORM

To whom it may concern:

This is to inform you of my recent marriage and to request a change of name and/or address. The following information will be effective as of: _____

My account/policy number is: _____

Under the name of: _____

Previous Information:

Husband's Name: _____ Phone: _____

Previous Address: _____

Wife's Maiden Name: _____ Phone: _____

Previous Address: _____

New Information:

Husband's Name: _____ Phone: _____

Wife's Name: _____ Phone: _____

New Address: _____

Special Instructions:

❏ Change name
❏ Change address/phone
❏ Add spouse's name
❏ Send necessary forms to include my spouse on my policy/account
❏ We plan to continue service
❏ We plan to discontinue service after: _____

If you have any questions, please feel free to contact us at: (   ) _____

Husband's Signature: _____

Wife's Signature: _____

CHANGE OF ADDRESS WORKSHEET

COMPANY	Account or Policy No.	Phone or Address	Done ✔
Auto Insurance			
Auto Registration			
Bank Accounts			
1)			
2)			
3)			
Credit Cards			
1)			
2)			
3)			
4)			
Dentist			
Doctors			
Driver's License			
Employee Records			
Insurance: Dental			
Insurance: Disability			
Insurance: Homeowner's			
Insurance: Life			
Insurance: Renter's			
Insurance: Other			
IRA Accounts			
1)			
2)			
3)			
Leases			
1)			
2)			
Loan Companies			
1)			
2)			
3)			

COMPANY	Account or Policy No.	Phone or Address	Done ✔
Magazines			
Memberships			
1)			
2)			
3)			
Mortgage			
Newspaper			
1)			
2)			
Passport			
Pensions			
Post Office			
Property Title			
Retirement Accounts			
1)			
2)			
Safe Deposit Box			
School Records			
1)			
2)			
3)			
Social Security			
Stockbroker			
Taxes			
Telephone Company			
Utilities			
Voter Registration			
Will/Trust			
Other:			
Other:			
Other:			
Other:			

WEDDING CONSULTANTS COMPARISON CHART

Questions	POSSIBILITY 1
What is the name of the wedding consulting business?	
What is the website and e-mail of the wedding consultant?	
What is the address of the wedding consultant?	
What is the name and phone number of the wedding consultant?	
How many years of professional experience do you have?	
How many consultants are in your company?	
Are you a member of the Association of Bridal Consultants?	
What services do you provide?	
What are your hourly fees?	
What is your fee for complete wedding planning?	
What is your fee to oversee the rehearsal and wedding day?	
What is your payment policy?	
What is your cancellation policy?	
Do you have liability insurance?	
Other:	
Other:	
Other:	

POSSIBILITY 2	POSSIBILITY 3

WEDDING CONSULTANT'S INFORMATION FORM

Make a copy of this form and give it to your wedding consultant.

THE WEDDING OF:

Ceremony Site: _____ Phone: _____

Ceremony Address: _____

City: _____ State: _____ Zip: _____

Website: _____ E-mail: _____

Reception Site: _____ Phone: _____

Reception Address: _____

City: _____ State: _____ Zip: _____

Website: _____ E-mail: _____

Ceremony Services	Contact Person	Arrival Time	Depart. Time	Phone Number
Florist				
Musicians				
Officiant				
Photographer				
Rental Supplier				
Site Coordinator				
Soloist				
Transportation				
Videographer				

Reception Services	Contact Person	Arrival Time	Depart. Time	Phone Number
Baker				
Bartender				
Caterer				
Florist				
Gift Attendant				
Guest Book Attendant				
Musicians				
Rental Supplier				
Site Coordinator				
Transportation				
Valet Service				

Timelines

THE FOLLOWING SECTION INCLUDES two different timelines or schedule of events for your wedding day: one for members of your wedding party and one for the various service providers you have hired.

Use these timelines to help your wedding party and service providers understand their roles and where they need to be throughout your wedding day. This will also give you a much better idea of how your special day will unfold.

When preparing your timeline, first list the time that your wedding ceremony will begin. Then work forward or backwards, using the sample as your guide. The samples included give you an idea of how much time each event typically takes. But feel free to change the amount of time allotted for any event when customizing your own.

This is a sample wedding party timeline. To develop your own, use the blank form in this chapter. Once you have created your own timeline, make a copy and give one to each member of your wedding party.

TIME	DESCRIPTION	BRIDE	BRIDE'S MOTHER	BRIDE'S FATHER	MAID OF HONOR	BRIDESMAIDS	BRIDE'S FAMILY	GROOM	GROOM'S MOTHER	GROOM'S FATHER	BEST MAN	USHERS	GROOM'S FAMILY	FLOWER GIRL	RING BEARER
2:00 PM	Manicurist appointment	✓	✓		✓	✓									
2:30 PM	Hair/makeup appointment	✓	✓		✓	✓									
4:15 PM	Arrive at dressing site	✓	✓		✓	✓									
4:30 PM	Arrive at dressing site							✓			✓	✓			
4:45 PM	Pre-ceremony photos							✓	✓	✓	✓	✓	✓		
5:15 PM	Arrive at ceremony site							✓	✓	✓	✓	✓	✓		
5:15 PM	Pre-ceremony photos	✓	✓	✓	✓	✓	✓								
5:20 PM	Give officiant marriage license and fees										✓				
5:20 PM	Ushers receive seating chart											✓			
5:30 PM	Ushers distribute wedding programs											✓			
5:30 PM	Arrive at ceremony site													✓	✓
5:30 PM	Guest book attendant has guests sign book														
5:30 PM	Prelude music begins														
5:35 PM	Ushers begin seating guests											✓			
5:45 PM	Arrive at ceremony site	✓	✓	✓	✓	✓	✓								
5:45 PM	Ushers seat honored guests											✓			
5:50 PM	Ushers seat groom's parents								✓	✓		✓			
5:55 PM	Ushers seat bride's mother		✓									✓			
5:55 PM	Attendants line up for procession			✓	✓							✓		✓	✓
5:56 PM	Bride's father takes his place next to bride	✓		✓											
5:57 PM	Ushers roll out aisle runner											✓			
5:58 PM	Groom's party enters							✓			✓				
6:00 PM	Processional music begins														

TIME	DESCRIPTION	BRIDE	BRIDE'S MOTHER	BRIDE'S FATHER	MAID OF HONOR	BRIDESMAIDS	BRIDE'S FAMILY	GROOM	GROOM'S MOTHER	GROOM'S FATHER	BEST MAN	USHERS	GROOM'S FAMILY	FLOWER GIRL	RING BEARER
6:00 PM	Groom's mother rises								✓						
6:01 PM	Ushers enter											✓			
6:02 PM	Wedding party marches up aisle	✓		✓	✓	✓								✓	✓
6:20 PM	Wedding party marches down aisle	✓			✓			✓			✓			✓	✓
6:22 PM	Parents march down aisle		✓	✓					✓	✓					
6:25 PM	Sign marriage certificate	✓			✓			✓			✓				
6:30 PM	Post-ceremony photos taken	✓	✓	✓	✓	✓	✓	✓	✓	✓	✓	✓	✓	✓	✓
6:30 PM	Cocktails and hors d'oeuvres served														
6:30 PM	Gift attendant watches gifts as guests arrive														
7:15 PM	DJ announces entrance/receiving line forms	✓						✓							
7:45 PM	Guests are seated and dinner is served														
8:30 PM	Toasts are given										✓				
8:40 PM	First dance	✓						✓							
8:45 PM	Traditional dances	✓	✓	✓				✓	✓	✓					
9:00 PM	Open dance floor for all guests														
9:30 PM	Bride and groom toast before cutting cake	✓						✓							
9:40 PM	Cake-cutting ceremony	✓						✓							
10:00 PM	Bride tosses bouquet to single women	✓			✓	✓							✓		
10:10 PM	Groom removes garter from bride's leg	✓						✓							
10:15 PM	Groom tosses garter to single men							✓			✓	✓			✓
10:20 PM	Place garter on woman's leg														
10:30 PM	Distribute flower petals to toss over couple														
10:45 PM	Bride and groom make grand exit	✓						✓							

WEDDING PARTY TIMELINE

Create your own timeline using this form.
Make copies and give one to each member of your wedding party.

TIME	DESCRIPTION	BRIDE	BRIDE'S MOTHER	BRIDE'S FATHER	MAID OF HONOR	BRIDESMAIDS	BRIDE'S FAMILY	GROOM	GROOM'S MOTHER	GROOM'S FATHER	BEST MAN	USHERS	GROOM'S FAMILY	FLOWER GIRL	RING BEARER

WEDDING PARTY TIMELINE

Create your own timeline using this form.
Make copies and give one to each member of your wedding party.

TIME	DESCRIPTION	BRIDE	BRIDE'S MOTHER	BRIDE'S FATHER	MAID OF HONOR	BRIDESMAIDS	BRIDE'S FAMILY	GROOM	GROOM'S MOTHER	GROOM'S FATHER	BEST MAN	USHERS	GROOM'S FAMILY	FLOWER GIRL	RING BEARER

SERVICE PROVIDER TIMELINE SAMPLE

This is a sample of a service provider timeline. To develop your own, use the blank form in this chapter. Once you have created your own timeline, make a copy and give one to each one of your service providers.

TIME	DESCRIPTION	BAKERY	CATERER	CEREMONY MUSICIANS	OFFICIANT	OTHER	FLORIST	HAIRSTYLIST	LIMOUSINE	MAKEUP ARTIST	MANICURIST	PARTY RENTALS	PHOTOGRAPHER	RECEPTION MUSICIANS	VIDEOGRAPHER
1:00 PM	Supplies delivered to ceremony site											✓			
1:30 PM	Supplies delivered to reception site											✓			
2:00 PM	Manicurist meets bride at:										✓				
2:30 PM	Makeup artist meets bride at:									✓					
3:00 PM	Hairstylist meets bride at:							✓							
4:00 PM	Limousine picks up bridal party at:								✓						
4:15 PM	Caterer begins setting up		✓												
4:30 PM	Florist arrives at ceremony site						✓								
4:40 PM	Baker delivers cake to reception site	✓													
4:45 PM	Florist arrives at reception site						✓								
4:45 PM	Pre-ceremony photos of groom's family at:												✓		
5:00 PM	Videographer arrives at ceremony site														✓
5:15 PM	Pre-ceremony photos of bride's family at:												✓		
5:20 PM	Ceremony site decorations finalized					✓	✓								
5:30 PM	Prelude music begins			✓											
5:45 PM	Reception site decorations finalized		✓			✓	✓								
5:58 PM	Officiant enters				✓										
6:00 PM	Processional music begins			✓											
6:15 PM	Caterer finishes setting up		✓												
6:25 PM	Sign marriage certificate				✓								✓		✓
6:30 PM	Post-ceremony photos at:												✓		
6:30 PM	Cocktails and hors d'oeuvres served		✓												
6:30 PM	Band or DJ begins playing													✓	

TIME	DESCRIPTION	BAKERY	CATERER	CEREMONY MUSICIANS	OFFICIANT	OTHER	FLORIST	HAIRSTYLIST	LIMOUSINE	MAKEUP ARTIST	MANICURIST	PARTY RENTALS	PHOTOGRAPHER	RECEPTION MUSICIANS	VIDEOGRAPHER
6:30 PM	Transport guest book/gifts to reception site					✓									
6:45 PM	Move arch/urns/flowers to reception site					✓									
7:00 PM	Limo picks up bride/groom at ceremony site								✓						
7:15 PM	DJ announces entrance of bride and groom													✓	
7:45 PM	Dinner is served		✓												
8:15 PM	Champagne served for toasts		✓												
8:30 PM	Band/DJ announces toast by best man													✓	
8:40 PM	Band/DJ announces first dance													✓	
9:00 PM	Transport gifts to:					✓									
9:30 PM	Band/DJ announces cake-cutting ceremony													✓	
10:30 PM	Transport top tier of cake, cake-top, etc. to:					✓									
10:40 PM	Transport rental items to:					✓									
10:45 PM	Limo picks up bride/groom at reception site								✓						
11:00 PM	Videographer departs														✓
11:00 PM	Photographer departs												✓		
11:00 PM	Wedding consultant departs					✓									
11:30 PM	Band/DJ stops playing													✓	
11:45 PM	Picks up supplies at ceremony/reception sites											✓			

SERVICE PROVIDER TIMELINE

Create your own timeline using this form.
Make copies and give one to each of your service providers.

TIME	DESCRIPTION	BAKERY	CATERER	CEREMONY MUSICIANS	OFFICIANT	OTHER	FLORIST	HAIRSTYLIST	LIMOUSINE	MAKEUP ARTIST	MANICURIST	PARTY RENTALS	PHOTOGRAPHER	RECEPTION MUSICIANS	VIDEOGRAPHER

SERVICE PROVIDER TIMELINE

Create your own timeline using this form.
Make copies and give one to each of your service providers.

TIME	DESCRIPTION	BAKERY	CATERER	CEREMONY MUSICIANS	OFFICIANT	OTHER	FLORIST	HAIRSTYLIST	LIMOUSINE	MAKEUP ARTIST	MANICURIST	PARTY RENTALS	PHOTOGRAPHER	RECEPTION MUSICIANS	VIDEOGRAPHER

WEDDING PLANNING NOTES

Wedding Traditions

HAVE YOU EVER WONDERED WHY certain things are almost always done at weddings? For example, why does the bride carry a bouquet or wear a veil? Or why do guests throw rice or rose petals over the newlyweds? In this section we discuss the origin and symbolism of some of the most popular wedding traditions.

THE BRIDE'S BOUQUET

In history, a bride carried her bouquet for protective reasons—carrying strong-smelling spices or garlic could help to drive away evil spirits which might plague the wedding. Eventually the floral bouquet became prevalent and symbolized fertility and the hope for a large family. Each flower was assigned a particular meaning when carried in a bride's bouquet.

THE BRIDE'S VEIL

The veil has historically symbolized virginity and innocence. It is believed that, in ancient times, a bride was veiled to protect her from evil spirits or to shield her from her husband's eyes. Arranged marriages were common and often they were not to officially meet until after the wedding.

RICE AND PETALS

The tossing of rice began to aid with fertility, both for the couple and for their harvest.

SOMETHING OLD, SOMETHING NEW, SOMETHING BORROWED, SOMETHING BLUE

Something old is carried to represent the history of the bride and ties her to her family. Something new represents the future and the bride's ties to her new family. Something borrowed should come from someone who is happily married and is carried in the hopes that their good fortune may rub off on you. Blue is the color of purity and is carried to represent faithfulness in the marriage. Many people don't realize that there is one more item—a sixpence in your shoe—which represents wealth.

WHITE AISLE RUNNER

Using a white aisle runner symbolizes bringing God into your union and is indicative of walking on holy ground.

SPECIAL SEATING FOR THE FAMILIES

The families are traditionally seated on opposite sides of the church, because in ancient times families would often have a wedding in order to bring peace to warring clans. In order to prevent fighting from taking place during the wedding, they were kept separate.

THE GROOM ENTERING FIRST

Traditionally, the groom enters first and gives his vows first, because he is considered to be the one who has initiated the wedding.

THE FATHER OF THE BRIDE WALKING DOWN THE AISLE

In historic times, brides were literally given away by their fathers—women were betrothed, often at birth, to men they did not know, and their parents were able to "give them away." Now, giving the bride away is simply a way for the bride's family to publicly show their support of the union.

THE BRIDE STANDING ON THE LEFT

Because ancient times were so violent and unpredictable, a bride was likely to be kidnapped and held for ransom at her wedding! The bride was placed on the groom's left in order to leave his sword-hand free in case he had to defend her.

THE SYMBOLISM OF THE WEDDING RINGS

The circle of the wedding ring represents eternal love and devotion. The Greeks believed that the fourth finger on the left hand has a vein which leads directly to the heart, so this is the finger onto which we place these bands.

KISSING THE BRIDE

During the Roman empire, the kiss between a couple symbolized a legal bond— hence the expression "sealed with a kiss." Continued use of the kiss to seal the marriage bond is based on the deeply rooted idea of the kiss as a vehicle for transference of power and souls.

THE COUPLE BEING PRONOUNCED "HUSBAND AND WIFE"

This establishes their change of names and a definite point in time for the beginning of the marriage. These words are to remove any doubt in the minds of the couple or the witnesses concerning the validity of the marriage.

SIGNING THE WEDDING PAPERS

The newlywed couple signs the wedding papers to establish a public document and a continuing public record of the covenant.

SIGNING THE GUEST BOOK

Your wedding guests are official witnesses to the covenant. By signing the guest book, they are saying, "I have witnessed the vows, and I will testify to the reality of this marriage." Because of this significance, the guest book should be signed after the wedding rather than before it.

THE PURPOSE OF THE RECEIVING LINE

The receiving line is for guests to give their blessings to the couple and their parents.

THE BRIDE AND GROOM FEEDING WEDDING CAKE TO EACH OTHER

This represents the sharing of their body to become one. A New Testament illustration of this symbolism is The Lord's Supper.

Wedding Party Responsibilities

EACH MEMBER OF YOUR WEDDING PARTY has his or her own individual duties and responsibilities. The following is a list of the most important duties for each member of your wedding party.

The most convenient method for conveying this information to members of your wedding party is by purchasing a set of the *Wedding Party Responsibility Cards*, published by WS Publishing Group.

These cards are attractive and contain all the information your wedding party needs to know to assure a smooth wedding: what to do, how to do it, when to do it, when to arrive, and much more. They also include financial responsibilities as well as the processional, recessional, and altar lineup.

This book is available at most major bookstores.

MAID OF HONOR

- Helps bride select attire and address invitations.
- Plans bridal shower.
- Arrives at dressing site two hours before ceremony to assist bride in dressing.
- Arrives dressed at ceremony site one hour before the wedding for photographs.
- Arranges the bride's veil and train before the processional and recessional.

- Holds bride's bouquet and groom's ring, if no ring bearer, during the ceremony.
- Witnesses the signing of the marriage license.
- Keeps bride on schedule.
- Dances with best man during the bridal party dance.
- Helps bride change into her going away clothes.
- Mails wedding announcements after the wedding.
- Returns bridal slip, if rented.

BEST MAN

- Responsible for organizing ushers' activities.
- Organizes bachelor party for groom.
- Drives groom to ceremony site and sees that he is properly dressed before the wedding.
- Arrives dressed at ceremony site one hour before the wedding for photographs.
- Brings marriage license to wedding.
- Pays the clergyman, musicians, photographer, and any other service providers the day of the wedding.
- Holds the bride's ring for the groom, if no ring bearer, until needed by officiant.
- Witnesses the signing of the marriage license.
- Drives newlyweds to reception, if no hired driver.
- Offers first toast at reception, usually before dinner.
- Keeps groom on schedule.
- Dances with maid of honor during the bridal party dance.
- May drive couple to airport or honeymoon suite.
- Oversees return of tuxedo rentals for groom and ushers, on time and in good condition.

BRIDESMAIDS

- Assist maid of honor in planning bridal shower.
- Assist bride with errands and addressing invitations.
- Participate in all pre-wedding parties.
- Arrive at dressing site two hours before ceremony.

- Arrive dressed at ceremony site one hour before the wedding for photographs.
- Walk behind ushers in order of height during the processional, either in pairs or in single file.
- Sit next to ushers at the head table.
- Dance with ushers and other important guests.
- Encourage single women to participate in the bouquet-tossing ceremony.

USHERS

- Help best man with bachelor party.
- Arrive dressed at ceremony site one hour before the wedding for photographs.
- Distribute wedding programs and maps to the reception as guests arrive.
- Seat guests at the ceremony as follows:
    - If female, offer the right arm.
    - If male, walk along his left side.
    - If couple, offer right arm to female; male follows a step or two behind.
    - Seat bride's guests in left pews.
    - Seat groom's guests in right pews.
    - Maintain equal number of guests in left and right pews, if possible.
    - If a group of guests arrive at the same time, seat the eldest woman first.
    - Just prior to the processional, escort groom's mother to her seat; then escort bride's mother to her seat.
- Two ushers may roll carpet down the aisle after both mothers are seated.
- If pew ribbons are used, two ushers may loosen them one row at a time after the ceremony.
- Direct guests to the reception site.
- Dance with bridesmaids and other important guests.

BRIDE'S MOTHER

- Helps prepare guest list for bride and her family.
- Helps plan the wedding ceremony and reception.
- Helps bride select her bridal gown.

- Helps bride keep track of gifts received.
- Selects her own attire according to the formality and color of the wedding.
- Makes accommodations for bride's out-of-town guests.
- Arrives dressed at ceremony site one hour before the wedding for photographs.
- Is the last person to be seated right before the processional begins.
- Sits in the left front pew to the left of bride's father during the ceremony.
- May stand up to signal the start of the processional.
- Can witness the signing of the marriage license.
- Dances with the groom after the first dance.
- Acts as hostess at the reception.

BRIDE'S FATHER

- Helps prepare guest list for bride and her family.
- Selects attire that complements groom's attire.
- Rides to the ceremony with bride in limousine.
- Arrives dressed at ceremony site one hour before the wedding for photographs.
- After giving bride away, sits in the left front pew to the right of bride's mother.
- If divorced, sits in second or third row unless financing the wedding.
- When officiant asks, "Who gives this bride away?" answers, "Her mother and I do," or something similar.
- Can witness the signing of the marriage license.
- Dances with bride after first dance.
- Acts as host at the reception.

GROOM'S MOTHER

- Helps prepare guest list for groom and his family.
- Selects attire that complements mother of the bride's attire.
- Makes accommodations for groom's out-of-town guests.
- With groom's father, plans rehearsal dinner.
- Arrives dressed at ceremony site one hour before the wedding for photographs.
- May stand up to signal the start of the processional.
- Can witness the signing of the marriage license.

GROOM'S FATHER

- Helps prepare guest list for groom and his family.
- Selects attire that complements groom's attire.
- With groom's mother, plans rehearsal dinner.
- Offers toast to bride at rehearsal dinner.
- Arrives dressed at ceremony site one hour before the wedding for photographs.
- Can witness the signing of the marriage license.

FLOWER GIRL

- Usually between the ages of four and eight.
- Attends rehearsal to practice, but is not required to attend pre-wedding parties.
- Arrives dressed at ceremony site 45 minutes before the wedding for photos.
- Carries a basket filled with loose rose petals to strew along bride's path during processional, if allowed by ceremony site.
- If very young, may sit with her parents during ceremony.

RING BEARER

- Usually between the ages of four and eight.
- Attends rehearsal to practice but is not required to attend pre-wedding parties.
- Arrives at ceremony site 45 minutes before the wedding for photographs.
- Carries a white pillow with rings attached.
- If younger than seven years, carries mock rings.
- If very young, may sit with his parents during ceremony.
- If mock rings are used, turns the ring pillow over at the end of the ceremony.

WEDDING CONSULTANT'S INFORMATION FORM

Make a copy of this form and give it to your wedding consultant.

PARENTS	Name	Phone
Bride's Mother		
Bride's Father		
Groom's Mother		
Groom's Father		
Other:		
Other:		

BRIDE'S ATTENDANTS	Name	Phone
Maid of Honor		
Matron of Honor		
Bridesmaid #1		
Bridesmaid #2		
Bridesmaid #3		
Bridesmaid #4		
Bridesmaid #5		
Bridesmaid #6		
Flower Girl		
Other:		

GROOM'S ATTENDANTS	Name	Phone
Best Man		
Usher #1		
Usher #2		
Usher #3		
Usher #4		
Usher #5		
Usher #6		
Ring Bearer		
Other:		

Who Pays For What

BRIDE AND/OR BRIDE'S FAMILY

- Engagement party
- Wedding consultant's fee
- Bridal gown, veil, and accessories
- Wedding stationery, calligraphy, and postage
- Wedding gift for bridal couple
- Groom's wedding ring
- Gifts for bridesmaids
- Bridesmaids' bouquets
- Pre-wedding parties and bridesmaids' luncheon
- Photography and videography
- Bride's medical exam and blood test
- Wedding guest book and other accessories
- Total cost of the ceremony, including location, flowers, music, rental items, and accessories
- Total cost of the reception, including location, flowers, music, rental items, accessories, food, beverages, cake, decorations, favors, etc.
- Transportation for bridal party to ceremony and reception
- Own attire and travel expenses

GROOM AND/OR GROOM'S FAMILY

- Own travel expenses and attire
- Rehearsal dinner
- Wedding gift for bridal couple

BRIDE AND GROOM

- Bride's wedding ring
- Gifts for groom's attendants
- Medical exam for groom including blood test
- Bride's bouquet and going away corsage
- Mothers' and grandmothers' corsages
- All boutonnieres
- Officiant's fee
- Marriage license
- Honeymoon expenses

ATTENDANTS

- Own attire except flowers
- Travel expenses
- Bridal shower paid for by maid of honor and bridesmaids
- Bachelor party paid for by best man and ushers

Wedding Formations

THE FOLLOWING SECTION ILLUSTRATES
the typical ceremony formations
(processional, recessional, and altar lineup)
for both Christian and Jewish weddings.

These ceremony formations are included in the *Wedding Party Responsibility Cards*, published by WS Publishing Group. This attractive set of cards makes it very easy for members of your wedding party to remember their place in these formations. Give one card to each member of your wedding party — they will appreciate it. This book of cards is available at most major bookstores.

$\mathcal{A}$LTAR $\mathcal{L}$INE $\mathcal{U}$P

ABBREVIATIONS

B=Bride	GF=Groom's Father	G=Groom	GM=Groom's Mother
BM=Best Man	BMa=Bridesmaids	MH=Maid of Honor	U=Ushers
BF=Bride's Father	FG=Flower Girl	BMo=Bride's Mother	RB=Ring Bearer
O=Officiant			

*P*ROCESSIONAL

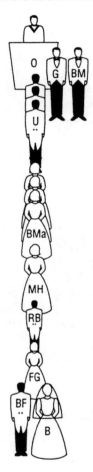

*R*ECESSIONAL

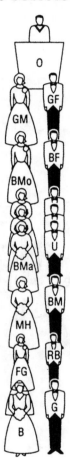

ABBREVIATIONS

B=Bride	GF=Groom's Father	G=Groom	GM=Groom's Mother
BM=Best Man	BMa=Bridesmaids	MH=Maid of Honor	U=Ushers
BF=Bride's Father	FG=Flower Girl	BMo=Bride's Mother	RB=Ring Bearer
O=Officiant			

*A*LTAR *L*INE *U*P

ABBREVIATIONS

B=Bride   GF=Groom's Father   G=Groom   GM=Groom's Mother

BM=Best Man   BMa=Bridesmaids   MH=Maid of Honor   U=Ushers

BF=Bride's Father   FG=Flower Girl   BMo=Bride's Mother   RB=Ring Bearer

R=Rabbi

$\mathscr{P}$ROCESSIONAL $\mathscr{R}$ECESSIONAL

ABBREVIATIONS

B=Bride	GF=Groom's Father	G=Groom	GM=Groom's Mother
BM=Best Man	BMa=Bridesmaids	MH=Maid of Honor	U=Ushers
BF=Bride's Father	FG=Flower Girl	BMo=Bride's Mother	RB=Ring Bearer
R=Rabbi			

RECEIVING LINE

HEAD TABLE

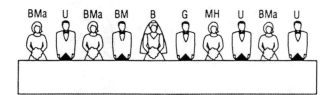

PARENTS' TABLE

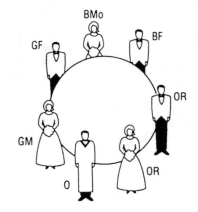

ABBREVIATIONS

B=Bride	GF=Groom's Father	G=Groom	GM=Groom's Mother
BM=Best Man	BMa=Bridesmaids	MH=Maid of Honor	U=Ushers
BF=Bride's Father	FG=Flower Girl	BMo=Bride's Mother	RB=Ring Bearer
O=Officiant			

Things to Bring

TO THE REHEARSAL

Bride's List

- ❑ Wedding announcements (give to maid of honor to mail after wedding)
- ❑ Bridesmaids' gifts (if not already given)
- ❑ Camera and film
- ❑ Fake bouquet or ribbon bouquet from bridal shower
- ❑ Groom's gift (if not already given)
- ❑ Reception maps and wedding programs
- ❑ Rehearsal information and ceremony formations
- ❑ Flower girl basket and ring bearer pillow
- ❑ Seating diagrams for head table and parents' tables
- ❑ Wedding schedule of events/timeline
- ❑ Tape/CD player with wedding music

Groom's List

- ❑ Bride's gift (if not already given)
- ❑ Marriage license
- ❑ Ushers' gifts (if not already given)
- ❑ Service providers' fees to give to best man or wedding consultant so he or she can pay them at the wedding

TO THE CEREMONY

Bride's List

- ❏ Aspirin/Alka Seltzer
- ❏ Bobby pins
- ❏ Breath spray/mints
- ❏ Bridal gown
- ❏ Bridal gown box
- ❏ Cake knife
- ❏ Going away clothes
- ❏ Clear nail polish
- ❏ Deodorant
- ❏ Garter
- ❏ Gloves
- ❏ Groom's ring
- ❏ Guest book
- ❏ Hairbrush
- ❏ Hair spray
- ❏ Headpiece
- ❏ Iron
- ❏ Jewelry
- ❏ Kleenex
- ❏ Lint brush
- ❏ Luggage
- ❏ Makeup
- ❏ Mirror
- ❏ Nail polish
- ❏ Panty hose
- ❏ Passport
- ❏ Perfume
- ❏ Personal camera
- ❏ Pen for guest book
- ❏ Powder
- ❏ Purse
- ❏ Safety pins
- ❏ Scotch tape/masking tape
- ❏ Sewing kit
- ❏ Shoes
- ❏ Something old
- ❏ Something new
- ❏ Something borrowed
- ❏ Something blue
- ❏ Sixpence for shoe
- ❏ Spot remover
- ❏ Straight pins
- ❏ Tampons/sanitary napkins
- ❏ Toasting goblets
- ❏ Toothbrush and paste

Groom's List

- ❏ Airline tickets
- ❏ Announcements
- ❏ Aspirin/Alka Seltzer
- ❏ Breath spray/mints
- ❏ Bride's ring
- ❏ Going away clothes
- ❏ Cologne
- ❏ Cuff Links
- ❏ Cummerbund
- ❏ Deodorant
- ❏ Hair comb
- ❏ Hair product
- ❏ Kleenex
- ❏ Lint brush
- ❏ Luggage
- ❏ Neck tie
- ❏ Passport
- ❏ Shirt
- ❏ Shoes
- ❏ Socks
- ❏ Toothbrush and paste
- ❏ Tuxedo
- ❏ Underwear

Wedding Calendar

THE NEXT SEVERAL MONTHS WILL BE FILLED with important dates. Make sure you allow yourself adequate time to book your ceremony and reception site in advance, schedule meetings with caters, photographers, florists, and bakeries—and still have time to take care of any other wedding planning details.

Use the 12-month calendar on the following pages to document your wedding date, parties, all of your appointments, scheduled payments, and any other items you want to complete by a certain date.

If you are planning on a health, fitness, and/or beauty regime during your wedding planning process, write down your routine on this calendar to keep you on track and help you reach your goal.

How to use the calendar: Assign the last calendar page provided for the month your wedding will take place. Then work backwards and simply fill in the month, year, and number of months before your wedding at the top of each page. Then fill in the dates based on each month.

WEDDING CALENDAR

Month:_____ 20_____ Number of months before wedding:_____

Sunday	Monday	Tuesday	Wednesday	Thursday	Friday	Saturday

Notes: _____

_____

WEDDING CALENDAR

Month:_____ 20_____ Number of months before wedding:_____

Sunday	Monday	Tuesday	Wednesday	Thursday	Friday	Saturday

Notes: _____

_____

WEDDING CALENDAR

Month:_____ 20_____ Number of months before wedding:_____

Sunday	Monday	Tuesday	Wednesday	Thursday	Friday	Saturday

Notes: _____

_____

WEDDING CALENDAR

Month:_____ 20_____ Number of months before wedding:_____

Sunday	Monday	Tuesday	Wednesday	Thursday	Friday	Saturday

Notes: _____

_____

WEDDING CALENDAR

Month:_____ 20_____ Number of months before wedding:_____

Sunday	Monday	Tuesday	Wednesday	Thursday	Friday	Saturday

Notes: _____

_____

WEDDING CALENDAR

Month:_____ 20_____ Number of months before wedding:_____

Sunday	Monday	Tuesday	Wednesday	Thursday	Friday	Saturday

Notes: _____

_____

WEDDING CALENDAR

Month:_____ 20_____ Number of months before wedding:_____

Sunday	Monday	Tuesday	Wednesday	Thursday	Friday	Saturday

Notes: _____

_____

WEDDING CALENDAR

Month:_____ 20_____ Number of months before wedding:_____

Sunday	Monday	Tuesday	Wednesday	Thursday	Friday	Saturday

Notes: _____

_____

WEDDING CALENDAR

Month:_____ 20_____ Number of months before wedding:_____

Sunday	Monday	Tuesday	Wednesday	Thursday	Friday	Saturday

Notes: _____

_____

WEDDING CALENDAR

Month:_____ 20_____ Number of months before wedding:_____

Sunday	Monday	Tuesday	Wednesday	Thursday	Friday	Saturday

Notes: _____

_____

WEDDING CALENDAR

Month:_____ 20_____ Number of months before wedding:_____

Sunday	Monday	Tuesday	Wednesday	Thursday	Friday	Saturday

Notes: _____

_____

WEDDING CALENDAR

Month:_____ 20_____ Number of months before wedding:_____

Sunday	Monday	Tuesday	Wednesday	Thursday	Friday	Saturday

Notes: _____

_____

WEDDING PLANNING NOTES

Honeymoon Planning

YOUR HONEYMOON IS THE TIME TO CELEBRATE your new life together as a married couple. It should be the vacation of a lifetime. This does not necessarily mean spending your life's earnings, but the vacation should reflect the special interests you share as a couple.

The honeymoon is traditionally the groom's responsibility. However, the planning of your honeymoon should be a joint decision as to where to go, how long to stay, and how much money to spend.

You will find tools and suggestions on the following pages to help you plan this important trip. After reading this book, you will have information on different types of honeymoons, and you should be able to determine the perfect honeymoon destination, research and select a responsible travel agent, gather useful information using the resource leads provided, establish a reasonable budget with confidence, and—most importantly—walk away with the assurance that you are planning the honeymoon of a lifetime! Start planning your honeymoon months before the wedding. Many locations that are popular with honeymooners tend to book fairly quickly, so the earlier you plan your trip, the better values you'll usually find.

There are many choices to make and many plans to be made, but most of them seem to fall into place once you've made the toughest decision — where to go!

Many people have a preconceived notion of where a honeymoon should take place. Indeed, year after year these locations are some of the places most frequently visited by newlyweds. We'll take a look at some of these "traditional" destinations as well as some that are a little less traditional.

Think about what you and your fiancé might find appealing (and unappealing) in the following honeymoon vacations. Be careful not to assume what your new spouse may be looking for in a honeymoon. Couples are often surprised when they discover what the other partner considers a "vacation." Refer to the section entitled Choosing a Destination to determine what each other's ideal vacation includes.

TYPES OF HONEYMOONS

Listed on the following pages are sample honeymoon plans—both traditional and less traditional. A brief description of some of the most popular honeymoon trips (ones that have remained popular with newlyweds for generations) is provided as well.

You can get very helpful information on planning a vacation package in the following brochures from the United States Tour Operator Association, (212)599-6599, www.ustoa.com.

- How to Select a Tour Vacation Package
- Worldwide Tour and Vacation Package Finder
- The Standard for Confident Travel

TRADITIONAL HONEYMOONS

Cruises

Cruises are a popular retreat for those who want the luxury of a hospitable resort with the added benefit of visiting one or more new areas. There are hundreds of different cruise options available to you. Typically, almost everything is included in the cost of your cruise: extravagant dining, unlimited group and individual activities, relaxing days and lively nights.

Costs vary greatly depending on the location the cruise will visit (if any) and your cabin accommodations. Locations range from traveling the Mississippi River to circling the Greek Isles. Spend some time choosing your cabin. Most of them are small, but pay attention to distracting things, such as noisy areas and busy pathways, that might be located close by.

Even though most everything is included in your cost, be sure to ask about those items which may not be included. Alcoholic beverages, sundries, spa treatments and tips generally are not included. Request a helpful publication entitled Answers to Your Most Frequently Asked Questions, published by Cruise Lines International Association, (212)921-0066, www.cruising.org.

All-Inclusive Resorts

Many newlyweds, tired from the previous months of wedding planning and accompanying stress, opt for the worry-free guarantee of an all-inclusive resort. Some resorts are for the entire family, some are for couples only (not necessarily newlywed), and some are strictly for honeymooners. Most of these resorts are nestled on a picturesque island beach catering to your relaxation needs.

Most offer numerous sports, water activities, entertainment, and exceptional service and attention. Your costs will vary depending on the location you choose, and there are many to choose from. "All-inclusive" means everything is included in your price. You won't have to worry about meals, drinks, tour fees or even tips.

One way of considering if this is a good option for you is to list all of the activities that the vacation package offers that you are interested in. Add up the individual costs and compare. If you wouldn't be participating much in the activities, food, and drink, you may actually save money by arranging your own trip at an independent resort. Even still, many couples prefer to spend the extra money in exchange for a vacation free of planning and wearying decisions.

Because of its convenience, many couples choose this resort option as the setting for their honeymoon. Some of the most popular all-inclusive resorts are Sandals and Club Med.

The Poconos

The Poconos Honeymoon resorts are located in Pennsylvania and are considered to be some of the most popular Honeymoon destinations around. The Poconos offer a variety of individual resorts, each heavily laden with fanciful symbols of romance and sweet desires. The atmosphere is perfect for those who want to be enveloped in a surrounding where you'll never forget you're in love and on your honeymoon. Some travel packages here are considered all-inclusive, but as always, be sure to ask about exclusions and extras. For information about honeymooning in the Poconos, call 1-800-POCONOS.

Walt Disney World

Another popular destination for those seeking a "theme" resort are those offered as Disney's Fairy Tale Honeymoons. These vacation packages include accommodations at Disney's exclusive resorts and admission to their theme parks. Some packages are also available with accommodations at some of the privately owned resorts at Disney World. Prices for Disney packages can range greatly depending on your tastes and the amount of activity you desire. For information on Disney's honeymoon packages, call (407)828-3400 or visit them online at www.disneyweddings.com.

Inquire with your travel agent about day or overnight cruises leaving from nearby ports in Florida. This is one way to combine two very popular honeymoon options into one!

Other Popular Traditional Honeymoons:

- Enjoying the beaches and unique treasures of the Hawaiian islands
- Exploring Northern California's romantic wine country
- Ski and snowboard package getaways in Vermont, New Hampshire, Colorado, and Northern California
- Camping and hiking within the beautiful and adventurous National Parks
- Sightseeing, touring, and exploring a variety of points in Europe via the rail system
- Island-hopping on a cruise ship around the Greek Isles

LESS TRADITIONAL HONEYMOONS

- Bicycling in Nova Scotia while relaxing at quaint bed and breakfast inns
- Participating in a white water river rafting expedition
- Mingling with the owners and fellow guests on an Old West dude ranch
- Visiting landmarks and parks while enjoying the convenience of a traveling home in a rented RV
- Mustering up the courage and stamina for an aggressive hiking tour of the Canadian Rockies
- Training for and participating in a dog sled race in the brisk tundra of Alaska
- Participating in a French or Italian wine country tour
- Enjoying an adventurous journey on the Orient Express
- "Roughing it" while enjoying the splendor of a safari in East Africa

HONEYMOON PLANNING NOTES

Choosing a Destination

MAYBE YOUR IDEA OF A PERFECT HONEYMOON is ten days of adventure and discovery; but for your fiancé, it may be ten days of resting in a beach chair and romantic strolls in the evening. The choices for honeymoon vacations are as varied as the bride and groom themselves. Deciding together on a honeymoon destination is a wonderful opportunity to discover more about each other and negotiate a vacation that will leave both of you relaxed, fulfilled, and even more in love.

First, determine the type of atmosphere and climate you prefer. Then consider the types of activities you would like to engage in.

Do you want the weather to be hot for swimming at the beach ... or warm for long guided tours of unknown cities ... or cooler for daylong hikes in the woods ... or cold for optimum skiing conditions? Keep in mind the time of year in which your wedding falls. Will you be escaping from extreme temperatures?

If you have a specific destination in mind, you (or your travel agent) will need to do some research to be sure the weather conditions will be suitable for your planned activities.

Review the previous chapters on traditional and nontraditional honeymoons and note what you feel are the pros and cons of each type of vacation. The two of you should have lots of images and possibilities in your mind at this point! The next step is to determine the most perfect atmosphere to provide the setting for your honeymoon. The following sections, "Creating a Wish List" and "Helpful Resources," will guide you through this next step and beyond.

CREATING A WISH LIST

Together with your fiancé, complete the Wish List worksheet. You should each check off your preferences, even if both of you don't agree on them. There are many locations that provide a variety of activities. Remember, you don't need to spend every minute of your honeymoon together, but your honeymoon destination should be one that intrigues both of you.

This worksheet is divided into 5 sections. You will be considering location, accommodations, meals, activities, and nightlife. While completing the worksheet, be as true to your interests as possible; don't concern yourself with finances and practicality at this point. This is your chance to let your mind wander! Think about what you would like to fill your days and nights with. This is the honeymoon of your dreams.

You step out of the plane, train, car or boat that took you to your honeymoon destination. You sigh with satisfaction at the memory of your flawless and enjoyable wedding as your feet touch the ground.

What type of overall atmosphere do you see yourself stepping into? What is the weather like?

Do you picture a long stretch of beach, towering mountains, blossoming vineyards, or city skyscrapers? Is the dry sand of the dessert blowing, or is everything captured under glistening snow caps?

Are there many people walking around (many locals, many tourists), or is it a secluded retreat?

 Are you relaxing indoors in a resort with a pampering environment that caters to your comfort, or do you return to a simple, modest hotel or motel after a long day of sightseeing, touring, and dining? Are you camping in the middle of your activities—hiking, climbing, fishing, etc.?

Do you see yourself interacting much with others? Would you like to have these activities be organized? Are there vistas and horizons to gaze endlessly upon, or is there an abundance of visual activity and changing scenery?

Are you enjoying exotic foods elaborately displayed and available to you at your leisure? Are you testing out your sense of adventure on the local cuisine and dining hot spots? Are you eating fast foods and pizza in exchange for spending your time and money on other items and activities that make your vacation exciting?

Are your evenings filled with romantic strolls or festivities that run late into the night? Are you staying in for romantic evenings or re-energizing for another busy day of honeymooning?

HOW TO USE THIS WORKSHEET

Each of you separately should place a check mark next to the items or images on the wish list that appeal to you. After you have finished, highlight those items that both of you feel are important (the items that were checked by both of you).

Next, each of you should highlight, in a different colored marker or pen, 2-3 items in each category that you feel are very important to you individually (even though the other person may not have checked it.

Your wish lists, after completing this exercise, will probably look like a list of all of the positive elements of all of your dream vacations combined. This is good; you should list as many things as you can think of. The more information you have, the better the suggestions your travel agent (or yourself if you'll be doing your own research) will be able to make.

Together, using this wish list, you will discover a honeymoon destination and match a honeymoon style that will fulfill your dreams. The resource leads and exercises provided in the rest of this book will help you get from wish list to reality. Happy planning!

HONEYMOON WISH LIST

Location	Bride	Groom
Hot Weather		
Mild Weather		
Cold Weather		
Dry Climate		
Moist Climate		
Sand and Beaches		
Lakes/Ponds		
Wilderness/Wooded Area		
Mountains		
Fields		
City Streets		
Small Local Town		
Large Metropolitan Area		
Popular Tourist Destination		
Visiting Among the Locals		
Nighttime Weather Conducive to Outdoor Activities		
Nighttime Weather Conducive to Indoor Activities		
"Modern" Resources and Service Available		
"Roughing It" On Your Own		
Culture and Customs You Are Familiar and Comfortable With		
New Cultures and Customs You Would Like to Get to Know		

Accommodations

	Bride	Groom
Part of a Larger Resort Community		
A Stand-Alone Building		
Lodging Amongst Other Fellow Tourists		
Lodging Amongst Couples Only		
Lodging Amongst Fellow Newlyweds Only		

Accommodations

	Bride	Groom
Lodging Amongst Locals		
Large Room or Suite		
Plush, Highly Decorated Surroundings		
Modestly Sized Room		
Modest Décor		
Balcony		
Private Jacuzzi in Room		
Room Service		
Chamber Maid Service		
Laundry/Dry Cleaning Service Available		
Laundry Room Available		
Beauty Salon on Premises		
Gym on Premises		
Gift Shop on Premises		
Pool on Premises		
Poolside Bar Service		
Sauna, Hot Tub on Premises		
Common Gathering Lounge for Guests		

Meals

Casual Dining		
Formal Dining		
Prepared by Executive Chefs		
Prepared by Yourself/Grocery Store		
Variety of Local and Regional Cuisine		
Traditional American Cuisine		
Opportunity for Picnics		
Exotic, International Menu		
Entertainment While Dining		

HONEYMOON WISH LIST

Meals

	Bride	Groom
Planned Meal Times		
Dining Based on Your Own Schedule		
Fast Food Restaurants		
Vegetarian/Special Diet Meals		
Delis, Diners		

Activities

	Bride	Groom
Sunbathing		
Snorkeling		
Diving		
Swimming		
Jet Skiing		
Water Skiing		
Fishing		
Sailing		
Snow Skiing		
Snowboarding		
Hiking/Rock Climbing		
Camping		
Golf		
Tennis		
Aerobics		
Sight-seeing Suggestions and Guidance		
Planned Bus/Guided Tours		
Ability to Go Off on Your Own		
Historic Tours		
Art Museums		
Theater		
Exploring Family Heritage		

HONEYMOON WISH LIST

Nightlife

Nightlife	Bride	Groom
Quiet Strolls		
Outdoor Activities		
Sitting and Relaxing Outdoors		
Sitting and Relaxing in Front of a Fireplace		
Being Alone with Each Other		
Being Out with the Locals		
Being Out with Other Newlyweds		
Discovering New Cultures and Forms of Entertainment		
Dancing/Nightclubs		
Visiting Bars/Pubs		
Theatre/Shows		
Gambling		
Concerts		

Other Important Elements

CREATING A WISH LIST

Now that you have created a wish list, take this list to your travel agent. If you don't already have a travel agent, use the following section to select a reputable agent.

A good travel agent, especially one who works with a lot of honeymooners, will be able to tell you about several different places that match your wish list while staying within your budget. (The section entitled Creating a Budget will prove invaluable in determining exactly what your budget will be.) Your travel agent should be able to provide a variety of options which contain different combinations of the elements of your wish list. Discuss with him or her which "lower priority" items you are willing to forego in order to experience the best of your "top priorities."

Helpful Resources

THE FOLLOWING PAGES INCLUDE HELPFUL RESOURCES that will come in handy when planning your honeymoon. Find information regarding travel agents and guidebooks, as well as websites and telephone numbers of travel bureaus from around the world.

TRAVEL AGENTS

Using the services of a good travel agent will take a lot of unnecessary pressure off of you. In the past, you may have felt you did not need the assistance of a travel agent when planning a vacation. Planning a honeymoon, however, can often be far more involved and stressful than a "regular" vacation, due to the simple fact that you are also deeply enmeshed in the planning of your wedding!

Therefore, you should take advantage of the professional resources available to you when working out the small details and finding the best values.

Keep in mind, though, that you will still probably want to do some research on your own, ask for second opinions and, most of all, read the fine print.

Since a travel agent can become one of your most valuable resources, you will want to consider a few important things when trying to select one. Ask family, friends, and coworkers for personal recommendations (especially from former honeymooners). If you are unable to find an agent through a personal referral, then select a few agencies that are established nearby from newspapers, phone books, etc.

Next, you will want to make an

appointment with an agent or speak to one over the phone. Pay close attention to the following and then make your decision.

Find out if they are a member of the American Society of Travel Agents (ASTA). Additionally, find out if they are also a Certified Travel Counselor (CTC), or possibly a Destination Specialist (DS).

ASTA: Members of this organization are required to have at least 5 years of travel agent experience. They also agree to adhere to strict codes and standards of integrity in travel issues as established by the national society. In most states, there are no formal regulations requiring certain qualifications for being a travel agent. In other words, any person can decide to call him/herself a travel agent.

CTC: Certified Travel Counselors have successfully completed a 2-year program in travel management.

DS: Destination Specialists have successfully completed studies focusing on a particular region of travel.

For a list of ASTA agencies in your area, call or write:

> American Society of Travel Agents
> Consumer Affairs Department
> 1101 King Street, Suite 200
> Alexandria, VA 22314
> (703) 739-2782
> www.ASTAnet.com

For a list of Destination Specialists and Certified Travel Agents in your area, call or write:

> Institute of Certified Travel Agents
> 148 Linden Street
> P.O. Box 56
> Wellesley, MA 02181
> (800) 542-4282 (press "0" to be connected to a Travel Counselor)
> www.ICTA.com

QUESTIONS TO QUALIFY YOUR TRAVEL AGENT:

- How long has the travel agency been in business?
- How long has the travel agent been with the agency?
- How much experience does the travel agent have?
- Any special studies or travels?
- Do they have a good resource library?
- Does the agent/agency have a variety of brochures to offer?
- Do they have travel videos to lend?
- Do they have a recommended reading list of travel aid books?
- Does the agent seem to understand your responses on your wish list and budget?
- Does he/she seem excited to help you?
- Does the agent listen carefully to your ideas?
  Take notes on your conversations?
  Ask you questions to ensure a full understanding?
- Is the agent able to offer a variety of different possibilities that suit your interests based on your wish list? Do the suggestions fall within your budget?
- Can the agent relay back to you (in his or her own words) what your wish list priorities are? What your budget priorities are?
- Is the agent prompt in getting back in touch with you?
- Is the agent reasonably quick in coming up with suggestions and alternatives? Are the suggestions exciting and within reason?
- Does the agent take notes on your interests (degree of sports, leisure, food, etc.)?
- Does the travel agency provide a 24-hour emergency help line?
- Are you documenting your conversations and getting all of your travel plans and reservations confirmed in writing?

Aside from just offering information and arrangements about locations and discounts, a good travel agent should also provide you with information about passports, customs, travel and health insurance, travelers' checks, and any other information important to a traveler.

OTHER SOURCES

National bridal magazines and general travel magazines are a great place to search for honeymoon ideas. But remember, you cannot always believe every word in paid advertising.

In addition to the information your travel agent provides, you can also obtain maps, brochures, and other useful items on your own. At the end of this section, you will find many useful phone numbers to help you in contacting tourist bureaus and travel agencies worldwide. These offices are extremely helpful in acquiring both general information (about weather, tourist attractions, landmarks, and even coupons or promotional brochures "selling" the area) and more specific information about reputable hotels, inns, bed and breakfasts, restaurants, etc.

Also provided in this section are phone numbers for sources specializing in information about traveling by train (in the United States as well as abroad) and for camping and hiking throughout the country.

The internet, your local library, the travel section of book stores, and travel stores are excellent sources for finding information and tips relevant to your travel needs. You will find books on traveling in general as well as books specific to the region or destination you will be visiting. There are numerous tour books, maps, language books and tapes, as well as books about a location's culture, traditions, customs, climate, and geography.

These books are a great source of information since they are independent from the locations they describe and are therefore impartial, objective, and usually contain correct, unbiased information. You can also find books and other resources describing (and sometimes rating) restaurants, hotels, shows, and tours. Books on bargain hunting and finding the best deals are common as well.

SOURCES TO READ

- *The Ultimate Guide to the World's Best Wedding and Honeymoon Destinations,* by Elizabeth & Alex Lluch
- The Stephen Birnbaum travel guides
- Frommer's guides
- Michelin Green Guides; Michelin Red Guides
- Insight Guides
- Let's Go! guides
- Fodor's guides
- Fielding's travel books
- *The New York Times Practical Traveler*
- *Mobil Travel Guide*

BACKGROUND NOTES

- **National Park Service Publications**
  (202) 208-4747
  www.nps.gov

- **National Forest Service Publications**
  (202) 205-8333
  A Guide to Your National Forests
  www.fs.fed.us

HONEYMOON PLANNING NOTES

Creating a Budget

YOU WANT YOUR HONEYMOON TO GIVE YOU luxurious experiences and priceless memories. But you don't want to return from your vacation faced with debts and unnecessary feelings of guilt for not having stayed within a reasonable budget. This should be the vacation of a lifetime. You can make this trip into anything your imagination allows. Pay attention to which experiences or details you would consider a "must have" and prioritize from there.

As you work with your budget, stay focused on those top priority items and allow less "elaborate" solutions for lower priority items. If you stay true to your most important vacation objectives, the minor sacrifices along the way will barely be noticed.

Perhaps, at this point, you don't know how many days your honeymoon will last. Often, the number of days you'll vacation depends on the type of honeymoon you choose. If you (and your travel agent) are designing your own honeymoon, the typical cost-per-day will most likely determine your length of stay. If you opt for a cruise or another type of prearranged vacation, your length of stay will probably be dependent upon the designated length of the travel package. By determining a basic, overall budget at the start, you will know what your limits are.

Yes, this is a very romantic time ... but try to remain realistic! Once you have an idea of your spending limits, your choices will be much easier to make.

Don't be discouraged if you're unable to spend an infinite amount of money on this trip. Very few couples are able to live life so carefree. You can still experience a honeymoon that will leave you filled with those priceless memories ... it's all in the planning!

The following budget worksheets will help guide you in creating your honeymoon budget. You may want to make copies of this worksheet so that you can create several budget plans. Keep trying different variations until you are satisfied with how your expenses will be allocated.

When comparing your potential honeymoon options, you'll find that laying out a simple budget is an effective and essential tool for making decisions.

GENERAL BUDGET

Traditionally the groom is responsible for the honeymoon. The groom will take on the challenges of gathering information and working through the necessary details of providing a perfect honeymoon for his new bride ... and himself! Nowadays, many couples find it necessary for both the bride and groom to contribute to the cost in order to experience the honeymoon of their dreams. (Today, the average newlywed couple spends $2,500-$3,500 on their honeymoon.) Many couples, together, determine what each partner will contribute and then shape the budget from there.

Some couples find that including the suggestion of a "Money Contribution Toward a Memorable Honeymoon" as a gift in their bridal registry is a great way for friends and family to contribute to the trip. Some couples also include some version of a "Dollar Dance" at their reception. This is a great way for the bride and groom to dance with many of their guests while accepting the dollar "dance fee" as a contribution to their honeymoon. Some couples choose to pursue less romantic options for building up the honeymoon savings ... part-time jobs, yard sales, etc.

Whatever your methods may be, remember that increasing the amount of money you will spend does not automatically ensure a more pleasurable and enjoyable vacation. Your most important and effective resource is your commitment to planning. You will see that, regardless of what your budget limits may be, your vacation possibilities are endless.

Note: Even if you think you have a good sense of what you will spend (or even if you plan on going with an all-inclusive package) going through this exercise is a smart way to ensure that there will be no surprises later on.

General Budget

Amount from the wedding budget
set aside for the honeymoon: $ _____

Amount groom is able to contribute
from current funds/savings: $ _____

Amount bride is able to contribute
from current funds/savings: $ _____

Amount to be saved/acquired by $ _____
groom from now until the honey-
moon date (monthly contributions,
part-time job, gifts, bonuses):

Amount to be saved/acquired by $ _____
bride from now until the honey-
moon date (monthly contributions,
part-time job, gifts, bonuses):

General Budget Total Amount: $ _____

DETAILED BUDGET

Before the Honeymoon

Special honeymoon clothing
purchases: $ _____

Bride's trousseau (honeymoon
lingerie): $ _____

Sundries (Helpful Hint: Make a list of $ _____
what you already have and what you
need to purchase. You can then use
these lists as part of your packing list):

Film, extra memory cards, camera $ _____
chargers, extra camera batteries:

Maps, guidebooks, travel magazines: $ _____

Foreign language books and CDs, $ _____
translation dictionary:

Passport photos, application fees $ _____
(see International Travel):

Medical exam, inoculations $ _____
(see International Travel):

Other items: $ _____

Before the Honeymoon
Total Amount: $ _____

During the Honeymoon

Transportation

Airplane tickets: $ _____

Shuttle or cab (to and from the $ _____
airport):

Car rental, gasoline, tolls: $ _____

Taxis, buses, other public $ _____
transportation:

Transportation Total Amount: $ _____

Accommodations

Hotel/resort room (total for entire $ _____
stay):

Room service: $ _____

Miscellaneous "hidden costs" $ _____
(Phone use, room taxes and
surcharges, chambermaid and room
service tips, in-room liquor bar and
snacks):

Accommodations Total Amount: $ _____

DETAILED BUDGET

During the Honeymoon

Breakfast: $ _____ per meal x _____ # of days = $ _____

Lunch: $ _____ per meal x _____ # of days = $ _____

Casual Dinners: $ _____ per meal x _____ # of days = $ _____

Formal Dinners: $ _____ per meal x _____ # of days = $ _____

Picnics, Snacks: $ _____ per meal x _____ # of days = $ _____

Meals Total Amount: $ _____

Entertainment

Sport and activity lessons $ _____
(tennis, golf, etc.):

Day excursions and tours $ _____
(boat tours, diving, snorkeling,
bus/guided tours, etc.):

Shows, theatre: $ _____

Lounges, nightclubs, discos $ _____
(don't forget to include the cost
of drinks and bar gratuities):

Museum fees: $ _____

Pampering (massages, spa $ _____
treatments, hairdresser, etc.):

Entertainment Total Amount: $ _____

During the Honeymoon

Miscellaneous

Souvenirs for yourselves: $ _____

Souvenirs and gifts for family and
friends: $ _____

Postcards (including cost of
stamps): $ _____

Newspapers and magazines: $ _____

Additional camera memory cards,
film, replacement sundries, other: $ _____

Miscellaneous Total Amount: $ _____

After the Honeymoon

Photo printing costs: $ _____

Photo albums: $ _____

After the Honeymoon
Total Amount: $ _____

For all-inclusive resorts/cruises and travel packages only

Fill in the entire budget form above (simply put a $0.00 on the items to be included in
the total package price). Then list the total inclusive package price on the line below.
Don't forget to include taxes and surcharges.

Inclusive Package Price: $ _____

DETAILED BUDGET

Detailed Budget Total Amount: $ _____

Doing a budget analysis may be one of the most useful things you can do in planning your honeymoon. With all the options available, a good cost analysis will help make the most appropriate decisions very clear to you.

First, create a budget using the above worksheet for what you think allows for an ideal, yet reasonable, honeymoon. Highlight those expenses which are top priorities. For example, a spacious, ritzy hotel room may be the most important element for you. Or, perhaps participating in numerous sports activities and excursions or enjoying fine dining is more important than a spacious room.

Next, as you come across different destinations and options that appeal to you, fill in a new budget worksheet. Compare the results to other potential trips. See how your priority items on each trip compare to one another. Determine the pros and cons of each. This is also an effective way of looking at the pros and cons of an all-inclusive package versus an independently organized trip.

Note: Once you've decided on your honeymoon destination and activities, fill in a new budget as accurately as possible and take it with you on your trip. Use it to chart your expenses as they occur so you will have a visual guide of whether or not you are staying within budget.

If you find that you are going over your budget, take a look at those top priority items that you'd still like to keep. See if you can eliminate some lower priority items to free up some money for the favored ones.

If you find you are under budget, celebrate with a special "gift" for yourselves (massages, an extravagant dinner, another afternoon of jet skiing, etc.).

Tipping Guide

THIS GUIDE IS PROVIDED TO HELP YOU get familiar with customary gratuity standards you may encounter throughout your travels.

Tipping customs vary from country to country. It is advisable to inquire about tipping with the international tourism board representing the country you'll be traveling in. Simply ask for information about tipping customs and social expectations. You will also want to discuss gratuities with your travel agent or planner. Some travel packages include gratuities in the total cost, some leave that to the guests, and some even discourage tipping (usually because they have built it into the total package price). Be sure to discuss this with your travel planner.

Air Travel

Skycaps .... $1 per bag
Flight Attendants .... None

Road Travel

Taxi Drivers .... 15% of fare (no less than 50 cents)
Limousine Driver 15%
Valet Parking $1
Tour Bus Guide $1

Rail Travel

Redcaps .... $1 per bag (or posted rate plus 50 cents)
Sleeping Car Attendant .... $1 per person
Train Conductor & Crew .... none
Dining Car Attendant .... 15% of bill

TIPPING GUIDE

Air Travel

Cabin Steward .... $3 per person per day

Dining Room Waiter .... $3 per person per day

Busboy .... $1.50 per person per day

Maitre d' .... At your discretion—recommended $10 - $20

Salon or Spa Personnel 15%

Bartender .... $1 - $2 per drink

Restaurants

Maitre d', Head Waiter ...... None (Unless special services provided, then typically $5)

Waiter/Waitress .... 15% of bill (pretax total)

Bartender .... $1 - $2 per drink

Wine Steward .... 15% of bill

Washroom Attendant .... $.50 - $1

Coat Check Attendant .... $1 per coat

Note: Some restaurants in foreign countries add the gratuity and/or service charge to your bill. If it has not been added, tip the customary regional rate.

Hotel/Resort

Concierge .... $2 - $10 for special attention or arrangements

Doorman .... $1 for hailing taxi

Bellhop .... $1 per bag + $1 for showing room

Room Service .... 15% of bill

Chamber Maid .... $1 - $2 per day or $5 - $10 per week for longer stays (no tip for one-night stays)

Pool Attendant .... $.50 for towel service

Miscellaneous

Barbershop .... 15% of cost

Beauty Salon .... 15% of cost

Manicure .... $1 - $5 depending on cost of service

Facial .... 15% of cost

Massage .... 15% of cost

Things to Pack

CONSIDER THE DIFFERENCES IN THE CLIMATES of where you live now and where you'll be visiting. Also consider the air conditions of airplanes, trains and boats. Bring along items that will help in the transition and keep you feeling as comfortable as possible.

Travelers' First Aid Kit

- ☐ Aspirin
- ☐ Antacid tablets
- ☐ Diarrhea medication
- ☐ Cold remedies/sinus decongestant
- ☐ Throat lozenges
- ☐ Antiseptic lotion
- ☐ Band-Aids
- ☐ Moleskin for blisters
- ☐ Breath mints
- ☐ Chapstick
- ☐ Insect repellent, insect bite medication
- ☐ Sunblock and sunburn relief lotion
- ☐ Dry skin lotion/hand cream
- ☐ Eye drops or eye lubricant
- ☐ Saline nasal spray, moisturizing nasal spray
- ☐ Vitamins
- ☐ Prescription or other birth control
- ☐ Physicians' names, addresses, and telephone numbers

PACKING CHECKLIST

❏ Prescription drugs
  Note: These should be kept in their original pharmacy containers that
  provide both drug and doctor information. Be sure to note the drug's generic
  name. You will want to pack these in your carry-on baggage in case the bags
  you've checked become lost or delayed.

❏ Health insurance phone numbers
  Note: Be sure to contact your provider to find out about coverage while
  traveling in the U.S. and abroad.

❏ Names and phone numbers of people to contact in case of an emergency

Carry-on Baggage

❏ Travelers' First Aid Kit (see previous section)

❏ Wallet (credit cards, traveler's checks)

❏ Jewelry and other sentimental and valuable items that you feel you must bring

❏ Identification (passport, driver's license or photo ID)

❏ Photocopies of the following important documents:

❏ Hotel/resort street address, phone number, written confirmation
  of arrangements and reservations

❏ Complete travel itinerary

❏ Airline tickets

❏ Name, address and phone number of emergency contact person(s) back home

❏ Medicine prescriptions (including generic names) and eyeglass prescription
  information (or an extra pair); list of food and drug allergies

❏ Phone numbers (including after-hour emergency phone numbers)
  for health insurance company and personal physicians

❏ Copy of your packing list. This will help you while packing up at the end of
  your trip. It will also be invaluable if a piece of your luggage gets lost, as you
  will know the contents that are missing.

❏ List of your traveler's checks' serial numbers and 24-hour phone number for
  reporting loss or theft

❏ Phone numbers to the local U.S. embassy or consulate

❏ Any "essential" toiletries and one complete casual outfit in case checked
  baggage is delayed or lost

❏ Foreign language dictionary or translator

❏ Camera

❏ Maps

❑ Small bills/change (in U.S. dollars and in the appropriate foreign currency)
for tipping
❑ Currency converter chart or pocket calculator
❑ Reading material
❑ Eyeglasses
❑ Contact lenses
❑ Contact lens cleaner
❑ Sunglasses
❑ Kleenex, gum, breath mints, and any over-the-counter medicine to
ease travel discomfort
❑ Inflatable neck pillow (for lengthy travel)
❑ Address book and thank you notes
(in case you have lots of traveling time)
❑ This book
❑ Your Budget Sheet

Other items to carry on

❑ _____
❑ _____
❑ _____
❑ _____
❑ _____

Checked Baggage

Clothing

Casual Wear
Consider the total number of each casual outfit item that you will need.
❑ shorts
❑ pants
❑ tops

PACKING CHECKLIST

- ☐ jackets/sweaters
- ☐ sweatshirts/sweatsuits
- ☐ belts
- ☐ socks
- ☐ underwear/panties & bras
- ☐ walking shoes/sandals/loafers

- ☐ _____
- ☐ _____
- ☐ _____

Athletic Wear

Consider the total number of each sporting outfit item that you will need.

- ☐ shorts
- ☐ sweatpants
- ☐ tops
- ☐ sweatshirts/jackets
- ☐ swimsuits, swimsuit cover-up
- ☐ aerobic activity outfit
- ☐ athletic equipment
- ☐ socks
- ☐ underwear/panties & exercise bras
- ☐ tennis/athletic shoes

- ☐ _____
- ☐ _____
- ☐ _____

Evening Wear

Consider the total number of each evening outfit item that you will need.

- ☐ pants or pants/skirts/dresses
- ☐ belts
- ☐ dress shirts/blouses

- ❑ sweaters
- ❑ jackets/blazers/ties
- ❑ socks or pantyhose/slips
- ❑ underwear/panties & bras
- ❑ accessories/jewelry
- ❑ shoes

- ❑ _____
- ❑ _____
- ❑ _____

Formal Wear
Consider the number of each formal outfit item that you will need.
- ❑ dress pants/suits/tuxedo
- ❑ dresses/gowns
- ❑ accessories/jewelry
- ❑ socks or pantyhose/slips
- ❑ underwear/panties & bras
- ❑ dress shoes

- ❑ _____
- ❑ _____
- ❑ _____

Other clothing items
- ❑ pajamas
- ❑ lingerie
- ❑ slippers
- ❑ robe

- ❑ _____
- ❑ _____
- ❑ _____

PACKING CHECKLIST

Miscellaneous Items

- ❐ An additional set of the important document photocopies as packed in your carry-on bag
- ❐ Travel tour books, tourism bureau information numbers
- ❐ Journal
- ❐ Special honeymoon gift for your new spouse
- ❐ Any romantic items or favorite accessories
- ❐ Extra film and camera batteries
- ❐ Plastic bags for dirty laundry
- ❐ Large plastic or nylon tote bag for bringing home new purchases
- ❐ Small sewing kit and safety pins
- ❐ Travel alarm clock
- ❐ Travel iron, lint brush
- ❐ Compact umbrella, fold-up rain slickers
- ❐ Handheld tape recorder (for recorded memory journal or for bringing along your favorite, romantic tapes)
- ❐ Video camera

- ❐ _____
- ❐ _____
- ❐ _____

For International Travel

- ❐ Passports/visas
- ❐ Electric converters and adapter plugs
- ❐ Copy of appropriate forms showing proof of required vaccinations/inoculations

Other items to bring

- ❐ _____
- ❐ _____
- ❐ _____

Items to Leave Behind
with a Trusted Contact Person

☐ Photocopy of all travel details (complete itineraries, names, addresses, and telephone numbers)

☐ Photocopy of credit cards along with 24-hour telephone number to report loss or theft. (Be sure to get the number to call when traveling abroad. It will be a different number than their U.S. 1-800 number.)

☐ Photocopy of traveler's checks along with 24-hour telephone number to report loss or theft

☐ Photocopy of passport identification page, along with date and place of issuance

☐ Photocopy of drivers license

☐ Any irreplaceable items

HONEYMOON PLANNING NOTES

International Travel

THERE ARE OVER 250 U.S. EMBASSIES and consulates around the world. After contacting the Tourism Bureau for the area you will be traveling to, it is also a wise idea to contact the U.S. Embassy or Consulate for that region. With assistance from both of these sources you will be able to determine the travel requirements and recommendations for your chosen travel destination.

Within this section you will find numerous resources to assure all of your questions and concerns are addressed before you travel. Call for a list of U.S. embassy and consulate locations with emergency phone numbers: (202) 647-5225 or visit http://travel.state.gov.

PASSPORTS AND VISAS

Your travel agent should be able to provide you with information to adequately prepare you for your international travels. Additional information (and possibly more detailed and current information) can be obtained by contacting the appropriate sources listed in this section.

As a U.S. citizen, you generally need a passport to enter and to depart most foreign countries and to reenter the United States. Some countries also require visas. A visa is an endorsement by officials of a foreign country as permission to visit their country. You first need a passport in order to obtain a visa. Inquire with the resources listed in this section for requirements of your specific destination.

As mentioned, you will be required to prove your U.S. citizenship upon reentry to the United States. If the country of your destination does not require you to possess a current passport, you will still need to produce proof of citizenship for U.S. Immigration. Items that are acceptable as proof of citizenship include a passport, a certified copy of your birth certificate, Certificate of Nationalization, a Certificate of Citizenship, or a Report of Birth Abroad of a Citizen of the United States. Proof of identification can include a driver's license or a government or military identification card containing a photo or physical description.

Note: The bride should have her passport and airline tickets reflect her maiden name for ease in proof of identification while traveling. Name changes can be processed after returning from the honeymoon with your marriage certificate.

Your passport will be one of the most important documents you will take with you. Contact the local U.S. Embassy immediately if your passport becomes lost or stolen. Have a photocopy of your passport's data page, date and place of issuance, and passport number to be kept with a contact person at home. You should also travel with a set of these photocopies in addition to an extra set of loose passport photos for speed in attaining a replacement.

Passports can be obtained from one of the 13 U.S. Passport Agencies (listed later in this section) or one of the thousands of authorized passport locations, such as state and federal courts as well as some U.S. Post Offices (check in the Government Listings section of your phone book).

Currently, the cost to obtain a passport is $65.00 (in person; Form DSP-11) or $55.00 (through the mail; Form DSP-82). If you have had a passport in the past, contact a passport agency to find out if you are eligible to apply through the mail. You will want to apply for your passport several months before your trip, keeping in mind that January through July is a busier time and the process may take longer.

In addition to calling the U.S. Passport Agencies for personal assistance, you can also call their 24-hour recorded information lines for information on agency locations, travel advisories and warnings, and Consular Information Sheets pertaining to every country in the world.

Travel Advisory Updates are also available 24 hours a day by calling The Department of State's Office of Overseas Citizens' Services at (202) 647-5225.

Additional, and very helpful, official information for U.S. citizens regarding international travel can be found at http://travel.state.gov.

Foreign embassies and consulates located in the U.S. can provide current information regarding their country. You can locate phone numbers and addresses in The Congressional Directory or Foreign Consular Offices in the United States, both available at your local library.

UNITED STATES PASSPORT AGENCIES

Website: http://travel.state.gov/passport_services.html
For all inquiries, call: 800-688-9889

Boston Passport Agency	Thomas P. O'Neil Federal Building
	Room 247, 10 Causeway Street
	Boston, Massachusetts 02222-1094
Chicago Passport Agency	Kluczynski Federal Building
	Suite 380, 230 South Dearborn Street
	Chicago, Illinois 60604-1564
Honolulu Passport Agency	First Hawaii Tower
	1132 Bishop St., Suite 500
	Honolulu, Hawaii 96813-2809
Houston Passport Agency	Mickey Leland Federal Building
	1919 Smith Street, Suite 1100
	Houston, Texas 77002-8049
Los Angeles Passport Agency	11000 Wilshire Blvd., Room 13100
	Los Angeles, California 90024-3615
Miami Passport Agency	Claude Pepper Federal Office Building, 3rd Floor
	51 Southwest First Avenue
	Miami, Florida 33130-1680

Seattle Passport Agency	Federal Office Building, Room 992
	915 Second Avenue
	Seattle, Washington 98174-1091

Seattle Passport Agency   Federal Office Building, Room 992
915 Second Avenue
Seattle, Washington 98174-1091

Stamford Passport Agency   One Landmark Square
Broad and Atlantic Streets
Stamford, Connecticut 06901-2667

Washington Passport Agency   1111 19th Street, N.W.
Washington, D.C. 20522-1705

Some private sources offering assistance in obtaining a passport
(usually with expedited service).

International Visa Service   800-627-1112
World Wide Visas   800-527-1861
Travel Document Systems   800-874-5100 or www.traveldocs.com

HEALTH CONCERNS

In the United States, the National Center for Infectious Diseases (NCID) and the Centers for Disease Control and Prevention (CDC) provide the most current information pertinent to international travel. The World Health Organization (WHO) concerns itself with general and specific health issues for almost every part of the world. Health and safety issues as related to international travel are the basis for the International Heath Regulations adopted by the World Health Organization.

Your travel agent should be fully informed about current conditions and requirements. Your personal physician should also be able to provide you with health-related information and advice for traveling in the region you visit. You can personally obtain very useful (and very thorough) information from the Centers for Disease Control and Prevention (CDC). The CDC's Travelers' Health Section has the following useful resources:

The Yellow Book, Health Information for International Travel
Order online at www.cdc.gov/travel/yb/

For updates and changes by phone or fax, call (404) 332-4559 or visit www.cdc.gov.

OTHER CONCERNS

Travelers' Health Insurance Coverage

If your health insurance policy does not cover you abroad, consider acquiring a temporary health insurance policy. Travel agencies, health insurance companies, traveler's check companies, and your local phone book should be able to provide names of relevant companies for you. In addition to health insurance coverage, many policy packages include protection in case of trip cancellation and baggage loss.

Keep prescription medications in their original pharmacy containers with the original labels. Bring a copy of your prescriptions and note the drug's generic name. You may consider getting a letter from your physician warranting your need for the medication.

Customs

The following list contains some useful publications regarding customs and custom policies when traveling internationally:

Know Before You Go: U.S. Customs and Border Protection Regulations for U.S. Residents
>   U.S. Customs and Border Protection
>   Available online at www.cbp.gov

An Unwanted Souvenir: Lead in Ceramic Ware
>   U.S. Food and Drug Administration
>   Available online at www.fda.gov

HONEYMOON PLANNING NOTES

HONEYMOON PLANNING NOTES

HONEYMOON PLANNING NOTES

DIY Wedding Projects

DO-IT-YOURSELF PROJECTS ARE A wonderful way to make your wedding day personal, special and memorable. They can also help you save money!

From arranging your own flowers to creating handmade favors, DIY wedding projects are a great way to cut costs and put a personalized touch on your Big Day.

In this section, you'll find 14 fun DIY wedding projects for crafty couples of all skill levels. Just be sure to give yourself enough time to complete each project, and always ask for help from friends and family if you need it. Enjoy!

DIY WEDDING PROJECT NOTES

Romantic Lavender Soaps

Delicate lavender buds and lavender essential oil make these handmade favors pop. You can wrap them in ribbon, raffia, or an organza bag, and voila!

Timeframe:
- 3 weeks or more before wedding date

Cost:
- $.50 - $1.50 per soap

What You'll Need:

- Clear Melt & Pour Soap Base
- White Melt & Pour Soap Base
- Light Gold Mica
- Ultramarine Violet Oxide
- Lavender Buds
- Lavender 40/42 Essential Oil
- 4-Lb Brownie Pan or Loaf Mold
- Microwave-Safe Pyrex Bowl
- Rubbing alcohol
- Small spray bottle

Romantic Lavender Soaps

TIPS & HINTS:

This recipe yields 9-12 fabulous wedding favors. For making large quantities of soap, keep in mind that 16 oz. of soap base makes roughly 4 bars of soap with your standard 4 oz. soap mold. Use 1/2 oz. of fragrance oil per pound of soap base.

STEP ❶: Melt about 16 oz. of Clear Melt and Pour Soap Base. Stir in 1/2 oz. of lavender 40/42 essential oil and about 1/2 tablespoon of light gold mica. Pour soap into your brownie pan or loaf mold. Spritz with rubbing alcohol to eliminate any bubbles. To avoid spots and speckles, mix your mica with a little rubbing alcohol before adding it to the soap base.

STEP ❷: For the second layer, melt another 16 oz. of Clear Melt and Pour Soap Base. Mix in 1/2 oz. of lavender 40/42 essential oil and 1/2 tablespoon of ultramarine violet oxide. Spritz the first soap layer with rubbing alcohol to help the two layers adhere. Pour the second layer and spritz again with rubbing alcohol to eliminate bubbles. Let second layer cool.

STEP ❸: For the third layer, melt 16 oz. of White Melt and Pour Soap Base. Mix in 1/2 oz. lavender 40/42 essential oil and 1/2 tablespoon of light gold mica. Spritz the second soap layer with rubbing alcohol to help the two layers adhere. Pour the third layer and spritz again with rubbing alcohol to eliminate bubbles.

STEP ❹: For the fourth and final layer, melt 8 oz. of Clear Melt and Pour Soap Base (you want this layer to be a little thinner than the other layers to really showcase the lavender buds). Mix in 1/4 oz. lavender 40/42 essential oil and between 1/4 and 1/2 cup of lavender buds. Again, spritz the third soap layer with rubbing alcohol to help the two layers adhere. Pour your fourth layer and spritz again with rubbing alcohol to eliminate bubbles.

STEP ❺: Let cool completely before cutting.

STEP ❻: Cut the lavender soap in any shape or size you want. Bramble Berry cut theirs with a crinkle cutter and finished by putting them in lavender organza bags.

DIY Project brought to you by:
Anne-Marie Faiola
Bramble Berry Inc.
www.brambleberry.com

Bird's Nest Seating Card Favors

These adorable bird's nest seating cards can double as favors for your guests to take home.

Timeframe:
- 1 - 2 weeks before wedding date

Cost:
- About $90 for 50 seating cards

What You'll Need:

- Miniature birds' nests
- Miniature egg-shaped soaps or candies
- White cover stock (80 lb. recommended)
- Ink pad
- Bird stamp
- Scrap paper
- Straight pins

Bird's Nest Seating Card Favors

STEP ❶: Fill each nest with three egg-shaped soaps or candies.

STEP ❷: While holding the contents in place, invert or hold the nest sideways. Then push a straight pin through the bottom of the nest up through each soap or candy to secure it in place.

STEP ❸: Using a dark-colored font, print guests' names on white cover stock approximately 1 inch apart vertically, one name per line.

STEP ❹: Cut each guests' name into a single strip of paper 1 inch tall. The length of the strip should be three times the length of the diameter of the birds' nests.

STEP ❺: Working over scrap paper to protect your work surface, stamp an image onto each name strip with a very light ink. You may want to do this off-center, so the focal point of the image appears beside the name.

STEP ❻: Wrap the guest-name strips of paper around the center of each nest. Secure the strips to the nests by pushing a straight pin through the nest where the ends overlap.

DIY Project brought to you by:
Betsy Pruitt
Belly Feathers Handmade Paper &
Party Goods
http://BellyFeathers.com

Aromatherapy Bath Salts Favors

Pure essential oils and natural Epsom salt makes for luxurious wedding favors that are simple to create.

Timeframe:
- 2 hours or less

Cost:
- $3 each

What You'll Need:

- Essential oils, .25 oz. with dropper (lavender, jasmine, ylang ylang, rose, or a blend)
- 6-pound bag of Epsom salt
- Ziplock bags
- Mugs, bowls, or decorative paper bags
- Cellophane wrap and ties (if using mugs or bowls)

Aromatherapy Bath Salts Favors

TIPS & HINTS:

A 6-pound bag of Epsom salt, found at any drugstore, should be good for 12 gifts. A .25 ounce-bottle of essential oils should yield about 300 drops. Look for pretty mugs or small bowls at the dollar store.

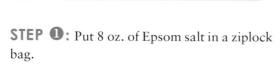

STEP ❶: Put 8 oz. of Epsom salt in a ziplock bag.

STEP ❷: Drop in 12 drops of essential oil.

STEP ❸: Zip up the bag and shake well to break up beads of oil.

STEP ❹: Once bath salts are complete, pour them into decorative containers, cover with cellophane wrap and tie off.

STEP ❺: If using a decorative paper bag, keep the bath salts in the plastic ziplock baggie inside the paper bag to prevent the oils from staining through.

DIY Project brought to you by:
Cher Kore
Kameleon Healing Aromatherapy
www.khealing.com

Photo credit:
© iStockphoto/Liv Friis-Larsen

Shrink Plastic Flower Pin

Flower pins in your wedding colors make whimsical boutonnieres for your groomsmen, or try a cluster on the mother-of-the-bride's lapel. They can even be a lovely accessory for place settings.

Timeframe:
- 1 hour for each flower

Cost:
- Under $30 for 10 flowers

What You'll Need:

- Two sheets of clear shrink plastic (www.shrinkydinks.com)
- Pattern of flower shapes
- Scissors
- Cookie sheet or toaster oven tray
- Racquetball
- Paintbrush
- Craft acrylic paint
- Craft acrylic varnish (gloss)
- Razor or X-acto knife blade
- E6000 glue
- Pins

Shrink Plastic Flower Pin

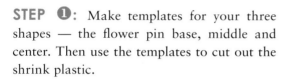

STEP ❶: Make templates for your three shapes — the flower pin base, middle and center. Then use the templates to cut out the shrink plastic.

STEP ❷: If your shrink plastic requires, sand one side of your plastic according to instructions.

STEP ❸: Shrink base piece first. Follow your shrink plastic instructions for heat settings and surface backing requirements.

STEP ❹: After the piece is entirely shrunk and lying flat, pull it out. Quickly, while it is still warm and malleable, form the piece around your racquetball to create a bowl shape. Be sure the shiny side is against the ball and the rough side is facing you. If you're unhappy with the shape, the piece can be re-heated and re-formed.

STEP ❺: Shrink middle and center pieces; form around the racquetball in the same way as the base piece.

STEP ❻: Paint each piece with craft acrylic paint. You can use one coat for a more translucent effect, or two for a more matte effect. Allow to dry.

STEP ❼: Paint each piece with craft acrylic varnish. Allow to dry.

STEP ❽: Use a dot of E6000 glue to secure the three layers together, and affix the pin back.

STEP ❾: Wear and enjoy! Make more!

DIY Project brought to you by:
Jessica Poundstone
Jewelry By Jessica
www.jewelrybyjessica.com
www.jessicapoundstone.etsy.com

Seashell-Embellished Programs

Natural elements like sand dollars and Japanese woven paper give a beachy, upscale feel to your ceremony programs or even your seating chart and dinner menus.

Timeframe:
- 1 weekend, 3 weeks before the wedding date

Cost:
- $5 each

What You'll Need:

- Cardstock (one 8.5 x 10 sheet per cover)
- Basho/Japanese Woven Cane Paper (one 24 x 36 sheet)
- Contrasting cardstock to back cane paper
- Rubber cement
- Hot glue gun
- Thin, satin ribbon
- Sand dollar shells (2 to 3")
- Stapler
- Program insert

Seashell-Embellished Programs

What You'll Need (cont'd):

- Paper trimmer with cutting and scoring blade

TIPS & HINTS:

Basho or Japanese Woven Cane Paper can be purchased online at sites like Paper.com and Kate's Paperie. One sheet will be more than enough for 25 programs.

STEP ❶: Using the paper trimmer, cut down the main sheet of cardstock to 5.5 x 11 to fold into a 5.5-inch program. To make a clean crease for the fold, use the scoring blade.

STEP ❷: Cut the cane paper into 3-inch squares and the contrasting cardstock into 4-inch squares.

STEP ❸: Use rubber cement to glue a 3-inch square of cane paper to the square of contrasting cardstock. Adhere that piece to the center of the cover.

STEP ❹: Affix a sand dollar to the center with a hot glue gun.

STEP ❺: Once dried and set, insert the program pages (cut down to 5.25 x 10.5, folded and stapled in the fold to secure together) and tie in place with the thin, satin ribbon.

DIY Project brought to you by:
Lori Decter
Married2MrWright on
ProjectWedding.com

Strung Flowers Wedding Altar

Add warmth and focus to a non-traditional space, such as a loft, restaurant or art gallery, by creating an altar out of ribbon, twine, flowers, and other natural materials.

Timeframe:
- 1 - 2 days before the wedding

Cost:
- $40 - $50 per strand for marigolds or a similarly priced flower

What You'll Need:
- Twine
- Floral wire
- Flowers, 6 to 9 per strand
- Dried leaves
- Ribbon
- Scissors
- Thumbtacks or ceiling hooks

Strung Flowers Wedding Altar

STEP ❶: Cut your twine to the length you'd like for your strand; about 2.5 feet long each.

STEP ❷: Take 6-9 marigolds or mums, cut the stems about 2 inches from the flower head and wrap them together with floral wire close to the flower heads.

STEP ❸: Affix the floral bundle to the twine using more floral wire. Repeat until you have the coverage that you'd like up and down the twine, leaving about 4 inches at the top of the twine free to tie to your satin ribbon. Trim any end of the stems that peek out as needed.

STEP ❹: Add bittersweet and dried oak leaves in the same way. Affix sporadically up and down the strand, being sure to balance the branches around the strand so that weight-wise the strand will hang straight down.

STEP ❺: Refrigerate strands until use.

STEP ❻: On the wedding day, cut a long piece of satin ribbon; the length will depend on your ceiling height. Tie the ribbon securely to the twine, making several tight knots. Trim twine as needed.

STEP ❼: Hang your strung flowers altar from the ceiling using thumbtacks or ceiling hooks.

DIY Project brought to you by:
Kathy Beymer
MerrimentDesign.com

Photo credit:
PenCarlson Photography

Fabric Ring Bearer Pillow

A handmade ring pillow makes for beautiful photos of the ring, your ring bearer or Best Man during the ceremony. Best of all, it's easy to make and customize with any combination of printed or solid fabrics you choose.

Timeframe:
- 1 month out from the wedding

Cost:
- $10

What You'll Need:

- Fabric/s to match your wedding theme
- Grosgrain, silk, or velvet ribbon
- Thread the same color as your ribbon
- Loose pillow stuffing
- Fabric scissors
- Sewing machine
- Iron

Fabric Ring Bearer Pillow

STEP ❶: Cut two pieces of fabric into 7 x 7-inch squares. You can either put the same fabric on the top and bottom of the ring pillow, or mix and match patterns or solids.

STEP ❷: With right sides together, sew a 1/2-inch seam around the pillow, leaving about 3 inches open.

STEP ❸: Clip corners. Turn the pillow right side out and press.

STEP ❹: Fill the pillow with loose pillow stuffing, making sure to tease apart the stuffing apart first to avoid it balling up inside. Slipstitch the opening shut.

STEP ❺: Cut a piece of ribbon long enough to tie in a nice bow, about 24 inches. Fold your ribbon in half and secure it with thread the same color as your ribbon. Go all the way through to the backside of the pillow, which makes a cute indentation on the back. Make about six or so stitches through to hold the ribbon securely.

STEP ❻: Tie a knot in the ribbon to cover up the stitches on the front. The finished pillow is a 6 x 6-inch square.

DIY Project brought to you by:
Kathy Beymer
MerrimentDesign.com

Photo credit:
PenCarlson Photography

Cross Stitched Reserved Signs

Hanging this hand stitched reserved sign on the back of the chairs at the head table lends a home-spun, personal feel to your wedding day. You might even create table numbers in this same style!

Timeframe:
- 1 day, a few weeks before wedding

Cost:
- $12

What You'll Need:

- Cross stitch linen material
- Cross stitch string and needles
- Wood veneer
- Heavy duty double sided tape
- X-acto knife
- Heavy duty glue
- Craft cutting mat
- String or ribbon

Cross Stitched Reserved Signs

STEP ❶: Purchase thin pieces of rectangle-shaped craft wood pieces (approx. 1/4-inch thick).

STEP ❷: Choose a font that you like that matches your wedding theme and type the word "reserved."

STEP ❸: Enlarge/shrink the font in a design or word processing program, making sure that it fits into the wooden rectangle.

STEP ❹: Print out the word.

STEP ❺: Lay the linen on top of the printed "reserved" to create an outline of the word on the linen.

STEP ❻: Cross stitch the word.

STEP ❼: Cut the word out of the cross-stitch linen (remember to leave room so that the edges of the linen meet the edge of the wood rectangle piece).

STEP ❽: Lay the linen cross-stitched word on top of the wooden rectangle and tape or glue the linen to the wood.

STEP ❾: Drill a hole through the wood rectangle in the top corners and the cross stitched linen.

STEP ❿: String your string or ribbon through the hole. Hang the sign on the backs of your chairs!

DIY Project brought to you by:
Laurel Smith
Laurel Denise Jewelry
www.laureldenise.com
www.laureldenise.blogspot.com

Photo credit:
Meg Runion

Paper & Fabric Flower Centerpieces

Colorful paper and fabric flowers embellished with vibrant feathers make for an eye-catching centerpiece that can save you money.

Timeframe:
- 4.5 hours per centerpiece, not including purchasing materials
- Start 6 months out for 12 centerpieces

Cost:
- $27 per centerpiece

What You'll Need:
- Centerpiece container
- Styrofoam ball , 6" ball
- 16-gauge floral wire (about 33)
- Floral tape
- White glue
- Paper and fabric
- Feathers or embellishments
- Needle-nose pliers with wire cutter
- Scissors

Paper & Fabric Flower Centerpieces

Making the Flowers

STEP ❶: Decide what you want your flowers to look like. Do you want the petals to be pointed, round, heart-shaped? How many petals do you want your flowers to have? Do you want to make one type of flower, or several? You can base your petals off of real life flowers, or make up whatever shapes you like.

STEP ❷: Once you have decided on your petal shapes, trace them onto plain paper. They should be about 2 to 2.5 inches in length. Cut out the shapes to use as a template.

STEP ❸: Using your templates, trace petals onto your various colored papers and fabrics, and cut them out.

STEP ❹: Using pliers make a small closed loop at the end of each wire. This will keep the petals from falling off.

STEP ❺: Wrap petals one at a time around the wire and secure with floral tape around base.

STEP ❻: To make leaves for your arrangements, cut your desired leaf shapes from the paper of your choice. If you want to, you can make a leaf template like you did for the petals. Dip the end of each plain wire into glue and lay flat on the backside of your leaves. Let dry. After the glue dries you can bend/curve the wire and leaves to make them look realistic.

Making the Arrangement

STEP ❶: Decorate the container you are going to arrange the flowers in. Paint the container or cover it with fabric or paper.

STEP ❷: Fit the styrofoam ball into the container, use glue as necessary so that it doesn't shift.

STEP ❸: Use wire cutters to cut the stems of the flowers, leaves and feathers to desired lengths, plus about 2-3 inches extra length.

STEP ❹: Insert flowers, leaves, and optional feathers (or other embellishments) into the styrofoam ball in your desired arrangement.

DIY Project brought to you by:
Lauren Karzag Fritz
Ruby Firefly, rubyfirefly.etsy.com

Photo credit:
Dia Rao Photography
www.diarao.com

Wedding Cake Soap Favors

These soapy wedding cakes are quirky and fun to make. You can even match them to the colors of your real wedding cake.

Timeframe:
- 3 weeks or more before wedding date

Cost:
- $.50 - $1.50 per soap

What You'll Need:

- White Melt & Pour Soap Base
- Clear Melt & Pour Soap Base
- White Tea & Ginger Fragrance Oil (optional)
- Wedding Cake Mold
- Non-bleeding colorant (any colors you choose)
- Eye dropper
- Microwave-Safe Pyrex Bowl
- Rubbing alcohol
- Small spray bottle

Wedding Cake Soap Favors

TIPS & HINTS:

This recipe yields 9 to 12 wedding cake soaps. For making large quantities of soap, keep in mind that 16 oz. of soap base makes roughly 4 bars of soap with your standard 4 oz. soap mold. Use 1/2 oz. of fragrance oil per pound of soap base. And, for extra sparkle, you can purchase mica to sprinkle into the soap base!

STEP ❶: Melt about 4 oz. of clear soap base by heating for 30 second increments in a microwave-safe pyrex bowl. Add a drop of colorant and mix together. With your dropper, fill each little flower on the wedding cake mold with your colored soap. Note that a little goes a long way when using the non-bleeding colorant! Let the flowers cool.

STEP ❷: Melt about 8 to 10 oz. of white melt and pour soap base. Mix in 1/4 oz. white tea and ginger fragrance oil.

STEP ❸: Let your soap cool to 120 degrees before pouring your second layer. If the soap does not cool to 120 degrees, it will melt your flowers in the mold. So make sure to control the temperature of your soap by heating in 30-second intervals.

STEP ❹: Spritz the flowers with rubbing alcohol before pouring the second layer to make sure the layers will adhere. Pour your second layer and spritz again with rubbing alcohol to eliminate bubbles. Let the soaps cool for 4 to 6 hours before popping out of the molds.

DIY Project brought to you by:
Anne-Marie Faiola
Bramble Berry Inc.
www.brambleberry.com

Blooming Birch Trees

Turn a blank ceremony space into a glittering forest with handcrafted birch trees to line the aisle or decorate during the reception.

Timeframe:
- About 12 hours for each tree
- Six months before the wedding

Cost:
- About $150 per tree

What You'll Need:
- Tree branches
- Large buckets
- Spray paint
- Plaster of Paris
- White silk flowers in several sizes
- Hot glue guns
- Lights
- Craft store moss
- Fishing line (optional)
- Crystals (optional)
- Pearls (optional)

Blooming Birch Trees

TIPS & HINTS:

To complete this intensive project, you will need a few friends or family members to help you!

STEP ❶: Prune or purchase tall tree branches, each about 9 feet in height. Strip the leaves.

STEP ❷: At a local nursery, inquire if they will give or sell you planting buckets for large trees. (This bride got them at no extra charge.)

STEP ❸: Spray paint the buckets gold or any color you prefer.

STEP ❹: Arrange the tree branches upright in the buckets and fill with plaster of Paris. To help shape the branches, wet them down from time to time to keep them pliable and from breaking. Allow the plaster to dry.

STEP ❺: Remove the white silk flowers from the stems and glue them to the branches using a hot glue gun.

STEP ❻: To add extra sparkle to the trees, you can glue mini pearls to the branches, or, using fishing line, string crystals and hang them from the tree branches.

STEP ❼: Cover the plaster at the bottom of the buckets with moss.

STEP ❽: Drape lights through the trees to make them glow.

DIY Project brought to you by:
Jenny Campbell
Carolyn Griesmeyer, STEM NYC
www.stemnyc.com

Sweetheart Mosaic Vase

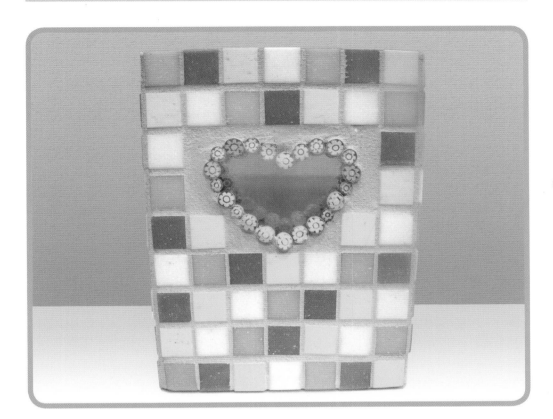

This lovely mosaic vase adds a pop of color and a personal touch to your wedding tables. Fill each vase with flowers or candles, or let them stand alone.

What You'll Need:

- Glass vase
- Mosaic tiles
- Millefiore (optional)
- Weldabond glue
- Grout
- Applicator
- Sponge

Timeframe:
- 2 months from wedding date

Cost:
- $35 each

Sweetheart Mosaic Vase

STEP ❶: Clean the glass vase.

STEP ❷: Begin adhering the mosaic tiles to the glass with the Weldabond glue — just a dab so that the tile is coated.

STEP ❸: Allow to dry at least overnight between sides.

STEP ❹: Mix the grout yourself (don't use the grout comes in a tube). Mix the powder with the water to get a consistency that's not too watery and not too clumpy.

STEP ❺: Apply grout to vase and smooth it over with a plastic applicator.

STEP ❻: After a few minutes, take a damp sponge and wipe off tiles.

STEP ❼: Allow to dry.

STEP ❽: Clean with glass cleaner. If you have grout on your tiles, scrape with a toothpick to remove.

DIY Project brought to you by:
Gina Florez
Minerva Invitations &
Announcements
http://minervainvitations.blogspot.com

Couple's New Address Bubbles

Ask your guests to see you off with these pretty bubbles, personalized with your new address as a couple. A wedding favor they can use!

Timeframe:
- 3 hours per 24 favors
- Several weeks before the wedding

Cost:
- $22 for 24 favors

What You'll Need:
- Miniature bubbles
- Sheer organza ribbon
- Patterned grosgrain ribbon
- Card stock
- 1" circle paper punch
- 1/8" circle paper punch

Couple's New Address Bubbles

STEP ❶: Using a word processing or design program, lay out the couple's new address in a ¾-inch area, leaving room at the top for the tag's hole. A decorative clip-art border can be added if the tag is slightly bigger than 3/4 inch. Copy and paste the address and border to fill an entire 8.5 x 11-inch page, keeping all of these 1.5 inches apart.

STEP ❷: Print addresses onto card stock using the printer's highest quality print setting.

STEP ❸: Using a 1-inch circular paper punch, cut out all of the addresses. Then using a 1/8-inch circle punch, poke a hole through the top of each tag.

STEP ❹: Cut sheer organza ribbon into 8-inch-long sections.

STEP ❺: Cut patterned grosgrain ribbon into 3-inch-long sections. Cut ends at opposite angles from each other.

STEP ❻: Tie organza ribbon around the bottle of bubbles right below the cap.

STEP ❼: Thread tag onto the right side of ribbon.

STEP ❽: Hold the grosgrain ribbon over the tag, and tie the organza ribbon into a knot to hold the grosgrain ribbon and tag in place.

STEP ❾: Adjust ribbons so that the grosgrain ribbon is angled with its left side highest. Adjust the organza ribbons at an angle with its right side highest.

STEP ❿: Trim edges of organza ribbon at opposite angles from grosgrain ribbon.

DIY Project brought to you by:
Betsy Pruitt
Belly Feathers Handmade
Paper & Party Goods
http://BellyFeathers.com

Succulent Love Place Cards

Hardy succulents lend a modern, organic, and elegant feel to these place cards, which guests will love to take home. Invite some friends to help you pot them, and make a day of it. Succulents also blend beautifully with traditional flowers for centerpieces and bouquets!

Timeframe:
- One hour per favor

Cost:
- $3.50 - $5 per favor

What You'll Need:

- Variety of 2.5" succulent plants (such as the Hens & Chickens variety)
- Small pots/containers approximately the size of the succulent pot
- Cactus soil (very important – don't use potting soil)
- Cardstock
- Glue or regal paper clips
- Spray bottle

Succulent Love Place Cards

STEP ❶: Design your place cards. You can purchase cardstock with a design that corresponds with your wedding style and write your guest's name and table number on each. Or, create a custom design in Photoshop, as in this example.

STEP ❷: Measure your container to decide on the size of your card. Cut out each place card and set aside.

STEP ❸: Begin potting your favors. Lay out all of the elements: succulents, soil, containers. Take the succulent out of the plastic pot. Use the pot to gather some soil and drop about 1 to 2 inches of soil into the bottom of your container.

STEP ❹: Nestle your succulent into the container and fill in soil around the edges to ensure all of the roots are covered and it's in there nice and secure. Repeat these steps for each of your succulent favors.

STEP ❺: Once all of your succulents are planted, use a spray bottle to give them all a nice light spritz. Let them dry.

STEP ❻: Before you attach the place cards, ensure that your succulents are dry so the water doesn't make the ink on your cards run. Put a dab of glue on the back of your place card and secure to the container, or use Regal Clips, as in the photo.

STEP ❼: If you're making the favors a week or so ahead of time, wait until just before the event to attach the place cards. That way you can give the succulents one more spritz of water before getting them ready for the big day.

DIY Project brought to you by:
Kelly Robinson Harris
succulentLOVE
www.succulentlovedesigns.com
Yes Please Designs
www.yespleaseblog.blogspot.com

Photo credit:
ErinHeartsCourt
www.erinheartscourt.com

WeddingSolutions.com

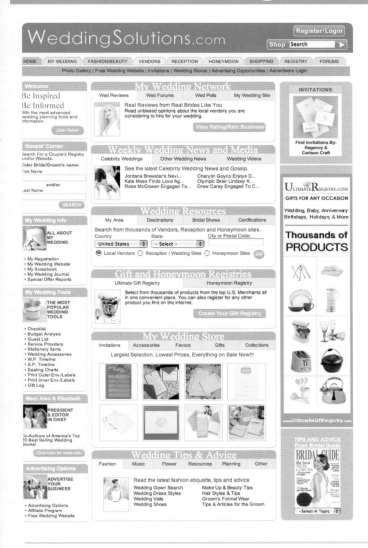

Everything You Need to Plan Your Dream Wedding

- The Latest Wedding Gowns
- Comprehensive Wedding Planning Tools
- Articles, Tips & Advice
- Thousands of Local Vendors
- Beautiful Reception Sites
- Honeymoon Destinations
- Largest Online Wedding Store
- Wedding Forums
- Personal Wedding Website
- Honeymoon & Gift Registry
- Polls, News, Videos, Media
- Wedding Planning Certification Programs

SEARCH FOR WEDDING GOWNS
View the Latest Designs

Search for your perfect wedding gown by designer, style and price.

SEARCH FOR RESOURCES
Reputable & Reliable

Find local vendors, reception, honeymoon & destination wedding sites.

Log on to www.WeddingSolutions.com for more information

WeddingSolutions.com

$99 Value

FREE Wedding Website on WeddingSolutions.com

Includes 19 Custom Pages

- Home
- Our Story
- Photo Gallery
- Details of Events
- Wedding Party
- Registry
- Local Info
- City Guide
- Accommodations
- Things to Do

- Restaurants
- Guest Book
- View Guest Book
- Sign Guest Book
- Wedding Journal
- Honeymoon
- Miscellaneous
- RSVP
- Contact Us
- Much More

SAVE UP TO $200 ON WEDDING INVITATIONS & ACCESSORIES

Invitations.......................

SAVE up to $100

- Wedding Invitations
- Engagement
- Bridal Shower
- Rehearsal Dinner
- Casual Wedding
- Seal 'n Send
- Save The Date
- Maps/Direction Cards
- Programs
- Thank-You Notes
- Much More!

Accessories.......................

SAVE up to $100

- Toasting Glasses
- Attendants' Gifts
- Unity Candles
- Aisle Runners
- Cake Tops
- Flower Girl Basket
- Ring Pillow
- Guest Book
- Cake Knife & Server
- Favors
- Much More!

Log on to www.WeddingSolutions.com/specialoffers for more details on these offers

ULTIMATEREGISTRY.COM

Create a gift registry for any occasion!

Choose from over one million products from the top U.S. merchants

- Gifts from the top U.S. merchants

- Compare products and prices

- Simplified notification process saves you time

- Same Merchants, Same Products, 1 Registry!

Already have everything you need or want?

Help those in need through our Charity Registry

Request that your guests donate much needed products to the charity of your choice in lieu of wedding gifts.

"Give a Gift" allows your guests to donate much needed products to the charity of your choice.

Your guests will be able to select from hundreds of national and local charities and see their "wish list" of the items they need most such as blankets, office supplies and more.

Your guests can then purchase these products in your name and they will be sent directly to the charity of your choice.

Log on to www.UltimateRegistry.com for more information